Health and Safety

Charity and voluntary workers

A guide to health and safety at work

HSE Books

Contents

Foreword *v*

Introduction *1*

Legal duties *3*

Managing health and safety and risk assessment *9*

Information, instruction, supervision and training *13*

Accidents, sickness absence and returning to work *17*

Charity shops *23*

Driving and transport *31*

Fire safety *39*

Fundraising *47*

Hazardous substances *55*

Lone working *63*

Moving and handling *69*

Work-related stress *77*

Violence at work *87*

Work equipment *95*

The workplace *111*

Appendix 1: Useful contacts *121*

Appendix 2: Relevant legislation *124*

Appendix 3: Forms *125*

Charity and voluntary workers: A guide to health and safety at work

Foreword

I am delighted to warmly welcome this updated guidance for charitable and voluntary organisations. As Immediate Past President of the Institution of Occupational Safety and Health (IOSH), itself a registered charity, I share its vision of a world of work that is safe, healthy and sustainable.

It is widely recognised that the voluntary sector makes a key contribution to the quality of life in local communities, as well as nationally and globally. Looking after the health and safety of everyone involved is an essential part of the work, and this guide should assist all who accept this responsibility.

All workers, both paid employees and volunteers, have a right to the efforts that are needed to prevent accidents and ill health – and have a personal duty to contribute. A sensible and practical approach to managing risks need not be burdensome. Much of this guidance is simple, requiring some basic thought, planning, consultation and good communications. This will benefit every voluntary organisation and help to improve the services provided.

Good management, including the management of risk, can only enhance the positive impact of voluntary work, and I commend this guide as a significant aid in this worthwhile effort.

Lawrence Waterman
Immediate Past President of the Institution of Occupational Safety and Health (IOSH)

I too welcome this guide. In working with the principal authors of the guidance I have recognised a strong desire to issue guidance that is as helpful as possible to those active in day-to-day charitable activities.

The worked examples here show the sorts of considerations that should be followed sensibly, and provided people take responsibility and use the guidance in this manner, good standards of health and safety can be more easily achieved across the charities sector.

Percy Smith
Principal Inspector
Commercial and Consumer Services, Transport and Utilities Sector
Health and Safety Executive

THANK YOU FOR YOUR SUPPORT • Please Give •

Introduction

About this book

1   This book is the result of a joint project between the Health and Safety Executive (HSE), the Charities Safety Group (CSG), and the Institution of Occupational Safety and Health (IOSH). HSE and CSG acknowledge the support and contributions made by these organisations, particularly Percy Smith (HSE) and Lawrence Waterman (IOSH). HSE would also like to acknowledge the contributions made by CSG members, particularly to Sarah Tullett (The Princess Alice Hospice), Garry Saunders (NCH, the children's charity) and Annetta Maslen (Croydon Social Services) for their work in redrafting this second edition.

2   This book aims to provide basic health and safety advice and information to charity and voluntary organisations. Many organisations, particularly smaller ones, do not have access to professional health and safety advice and simply do not know what it is that they need to know. This book aims to help them to find out and gives practical suggestions on how to work safely. It should also be of use to health and safety practitioners working in this specialised sector. The book covers the main aspects of health and safety that most charity and voluntary organisations will need to be aware of in order to meet their legal duties.

3   Each chapter looks at a specific health and safety subject and gives a general introduction to that subject followed by a series of practical case studies taken from actual events.

4   The term 'worker' is used throughout this book and deliberately includes employees and voluntary workers, ie people who work for an employer but not as an employee. While most health and safety law specifically refers to 'employees' and the duties owed to them, it is good practice, and very strongly recommended, that people working as volunteers are given the same level of protection as employees. Where the term 'employee' is used, this is deliberate and highlights specific legal points.

Charities Safety Group

5   The Charities Safety Group (CSG) was founded in 1997 to provide a forum for people with health and safety responsibilities, working in charity and voluntary organisations, to network and share information. CSG also represents the charity and voluntary sector in health and safety matters with HSE and other health and safety bodies.

6   Further information on CSG activities and membership can be found on the CSG website: www.csg.org.uk.

Further information

7   Information that is available in more detailed HSE guidance is not repeated in this book, but relevant publications are signposted and listed for further reference.

8   HSE has also produced a training video package that will support the information given in this book. The video contains three scenarios (a charity shop, a lone worker visiting a client at home and a fundraising fête), which are used to introduce the principles of risk assessment. The book and video are available individually from HSE Books.

9   HSE priced and free publications are available by mail order from HSE Books (see Appendix 1: *Useful contacts*). HSE priced publications are also available from bookshops and free leaflets can be downloaded from the HSE website: www.hse.gov.uk.

Legal duties

10   Health and safety at work are controlled by a number of laws, many of which come from European Directives. UK health and safety laws set out general requirements that can be applied to all workplaces, regardless of the type of work carried out.

Criminal law

11   Health and safety laws are part of the criminal law system. For example, all health and safety prosecutions in England and Wales are first heard in Magistrates' Courts, with the serious cases being passed on to the Crown Courts – juries may be involved in Crown Court cases. Successful prosecutions for failing to comply with health and safety laws may result in fines and court costs being placed on the defendant. In some cases, prison sentences may also be given.

Enforcement

12   The enforcing authorities for health and safety laws are HSE and/or local authorities, depending on the type of work carried out at the workplace.

13   The enforcing authority for industrial workplaces (such as factories, construction sites and farms etc) is HSE. HSE also inspects schools and hospitals.

14   Local authorities enforce health and safety in non-industrial workplaces (such as offices, shops, residential homes, hotels and restaurants etc). This is usually carried out by local council environmental health officers (EHOs).

15   Details of the enforcing authority for your workplace should be written onto the poster *Health and safety law: What you should know*, which you are required to display in your workplace if there any employees. See paragraphs 30-32.

Civil law

16   Civil law is also important in health and safety and mainly applies when a person injured at work claims compensation for their injury from their employer. Very simply, civil law is based on the principle of 'duty of care', ie everyone has a duty of care to everyone else. The claim for compensation is often (but not always) based on negligence by the employer (ie the employer has broken the 'duty of care') and that this negligence resulted in the injury.

17   Personal injury cases are taken through the civil (High) courts and may result in successful compensation claims reaching many hundred of thousands of pounds.

18   Personal injury compensation payments are covered by employers' liability insurance, which all businesses are required to have by law. While the employers' liability insurance policy is designed to cover these compensation claims, annual employer premiums will rise if claims are made against the insurance. In a worst-case scenario, insurance companies could refuse to insure employers with a poor health and safety record. Volunteer workers injured at work may also take a personal injury claim against the employer.

Insurance

19   Employers must consider a range of relevant insurances, depending on their work activities. Most charity and voluntary organisations will probably have the following insurance policies:

- employers' liability insurance (see paragraph 18) for personal injury claims;
- public liability insurance, for claims made by the public against the charity. This will also be relevant at any public fundraising events;
- vehicle insurance for company vehicles;
- some form of indemnity insurance, eg for professional indemnity.

UK health and safety law

20   The main law controlling health and safety at work in the UK is the Health and Safety at Work etc Act 1974 (HSW Act). This places general duties on employers to ensure the health and safety of their employees and anyone else who may be harmed by the employer's work activities or workplace.

21   To comply with these general duties, employers must, **so far as is reasonably practicable**, provide:

- safe equipment;
- safe substances;
- necessary information, instruction, supervision and training;
- a safe and healthy workplace;
- a safe and healthy working environment.

22   The term 'so far as is reasonably practicable' means that employers may balance the level of risk of harm against the cost (in money, time and other resources) of removing or controlling that risk. For example, it would not be reasonably practicable to spend millions of pounds controlling a low-level risk, ie a risk that is unlikely to happen and even if it did would not cause an injury or other harm.

23   The HSW Act also places duties on employees to:

- ensure their own health and safety and that of others who may be affected by their work;
- co-operate with their employer in health and safety matters;
- not misuse or interfere with items provided for health and safety reasons, eg using fire extinguishers to hold open fire doors.

24   Designers and manufacturers have a duty to provide safe equipment and substances intended for use at work and to provide relevant safety information about their products.

Regulations

25   The HSW Act is supported by many regulations setting out more detailed legal duties. The Management of Health and Safety at Work Regulations 1999 complement the general HSW Act duties above. In summary, they require employers to:

- carry out risk assessments of their work activities and workplaces – there is a specific duty to carry out risk assessments for young workers (ie under 18 years of age) and for new and expectant mothers (ie women who are pregnant or who have recently given birth);
- follow the 'prevention principles' for removing or controlling risks;
- have effective health and safety arrangements in place for managing health and safety (including emergency arrangements) and access to competent health and safety advice;
- take a worker's capabilities into account when assigning jobs;
- co-operate and co-ordinate health and safety with other employers, eg on shared premises.

26   Health and safety regulations often cover one specific topic, eg the Electricity at Work Regulations 1989, the Control of Substances Hazardous to Health Regulations 2002 (COSHH) etc. The following chapters will mention any relevant legislation and where more information can be found.

Approved codes of practice and guidance

27   HSE has produced approved codes of practice (ACOPs) and/or guidance for many of the health and safety regulations.

28   ACOPs are not law but can be used in court cases as representing the required legal standard. You do not have to follow an ACOP, but if you don't, you must meet the standards in some other way.

29   Guidance notes contain simple information on what the regulations require you to do.

Health and safety law poster

30 Employers are required to display the poster *Health and safety law: What you should know* in the workplace and bring it to employees' attention. It should be in a position where your employees can see and read it. If you do not want to display the poster, you may give each of your employees an individual leaflet that contains the same information. Good practice recommends that the poster should also be brought to the attention of volunteers.

31 The poster contains a summary of the main health and safety legal duties and provides spaces for certain information to be filled in.

32 The information that you have to fill in is:

- the name of the competent person responsible for health and safety;
- the names of safety representatives;
- the name, address and phone number of the enforcing authority for the workplace;
- the name and address of the local Employment Medical Advisory Service (EMAS) – this will be the address of your local HSE office, even if your workplace is enforced by EHOs.

Other legal duties you need to know about

33 As well as the general duties above and those covered in this book, you need to be aware of two more legal duties that relate to all workplaces.

Consultation
34 Employers are required to consult with their employees on health and safety matters. This may be through appointed, official union safety representatives (where the employer recognises that union) or through elected employee safety representatives for non-union workers. You may hear the term 'safety representative' to cover both types of representatives. Good practice recommends that volunteers should also be involved in the consultation process.

35 The laws covering consultation are the Safety Representatives and Safety Committees Regulations 1977, which cover consultation with workers who are union members, and the Health and Safety (Consultation with Employees) Regulations 1996, which cover consultation with workers who are not union members.

36 Both sets of Regulations define what the employer must consult on. Generally this can be summarised as:

- risks associated with the work activities and workplace and the necessary control measures;
- the introduction of any changes that may affect health and safety, eg new equipment, different work patterns or shifts.

37 Both types of safety representatives have defined roles. Union safety representatives have slightly more legal rights, ie they may:

- view relevant health and safety documents (but not confidential medical information), eg risk assessments, accident figures;
- talk to workers about health and safety;
- talk to enforcement officers during their inspections;
- inspect the work area they represent and submit reports;
- consult with their employer about health and safety issues;
- request that a health and safety committee is set up (two safety representatives must make this request) and attend meetings.

38 While the list of rights in paragraph 37 covers more than what is required for non-union safety representatives, it is good practice for both types of safety representatives to have the same rights in the workplace.

39 The Unison and Amicus unions have 'charity' sections that are able to provide support and advice, including the role and rights of union safety representatives – see Appendix 1: *Useful contacts*.

First aid

40 The provision of first aid at work is covered by the Health and Safety (First-Aid) Regulations 1981. These Regulations require employers to provide first-aid kits, other equipment and trained first aiders or appointed people for employees at work. Good practice recommends that first-aid provision is available to all workers at work.

41 What first-aid equipment you provide should be based on:

- the type of work carried out, ie **high** risk (eg use of dangerous machinery) or **lower** risk (eg office work);
- where the work is carried out, eg remote locations, lone working etc;
- the layout of the workplace, eg workplaces spread over a large area;
- the findings of your risk assessments, which will identify any problem areas where accidents are more likely to occur;
- the number of workers.

First-aid equipment

42 In most cases, this will be a suitably sized first-aid kit(s), located in an obvious and accessible place and clearly marked. First-aid equipment suppliers will be able to advise on the appropriate sized kit for your number of workers.

43 You will also need to think about providing first-aid kits for lone workers or workers who drive as part of their work.

44 Whatever the kit size, they will generally contain:

- assorted-sized plasters (blue or green for catering);
- a range of sterile dressings;
- eye pads;
- various bandages;
- safety pins;
- disposable gloves.

45 They must **not** contain any form of medication, including, for example, headache pills or anti-histamine tablets etc.

46 You will need a system to ensure any used items are replaced.

47 Workplaces with a large number of workers and/or where the work activities are specialised or high risk may require additional facilities, such as a designated and fitted out first-aid room.

First aiders

48 You must also provide trained first aiders to give first-aid treatment. First aiders must pass an HSE-approved four-day course and be available for the whole time people are at work, eg 24-hour activities such as care work. The certificate lasts for three years and must then be renewed. If the work activities involve special hazards, the first aiders may need specialised training.

49 Workplaces with very few workers and **low** risk activities may have appointed people instead of trained first aiders. These people have responsibility for getting medical assistance in the event of any accident at work. They may have attended an emergency first-aid course but cannot give the full range of first-aid treatments.

Competence and competent people

50 Health and safety laws often refer to the use of 'competent persons'. This term is not specifically defined but is recognised as:

a person who has the mixture and balance of knowledge, experience, skills and, if relevant, qualifications, to do their work safely and without risks to health.

51 A good example is the use of fully trained and registered electricians. There are some tasks, such as wiring a plug, which can be safely carried out by most people. However, you will need a competent electrician for more complex tasks such as working on an electrical installation. In all cases, make sure people are competent to carry out electrical work.

52 Most professions have an associated 'professional body' that sets standards of work and codes of conduct etc – they will be able to confirm if a contractor or your competent person is a registered member and meets their professional criteria.

Further information

Essentials of health and safety at work (Fourth edition) HSE Books 2006 0 7176 6179 2

An introduction to health and safety: Health and safety in small businesses Leaflet INDG259(rev1) HSE Books 2003 (single copy free)

First aid at work. The Health and Safety (First Aid) Regulations 1981. Approved Code of Practice and guidance L74 HSE Books 1997 ISBN 0 7176 1050 0

First aid at work: Your questions answered Leaflet INDG214 HSE Books 1997 (single copy free or priced packs of 15 ISBN 0 7176 1074 8)

The Employment Medical Advisory Service and you Leaflet HSE5(rev1) HSE Books 2000 (single copy free)

Employers' Liability (Compulsory Insurance) Act 1969: A guide for employers Leaflet HSE40(rev1) HSE Books 2006 (single copy free)

Consulting employees on health and safety: A guide to the law Leaflet INDG232 HSE Books 1996 (single copy free or priced packs of 15 ISBN 0 7176 1615 0)

What to expect when a health and safety inspector calls: A brief guide for businesses, employees and their representatives Leaflet HSC14 HSE Books 1998 (single copy free)

Managing health and safety and risk assessment

53 Health and safety has to be managed in the same way as any other business activity. Risk assessment is part of managing health and safety.

Managing health and safety

54 It is helpful to have a health and safety policy. Write down what you want to achieve, and how you intend to achieve it. This should include how you will communicate health and safety to your workers, and what everyone's responsibilities are.

55 Your policy should also include targets, which must be realistic, measurable and achievable. Measure your health and safety performance to see whether you have met your targets; if you haven't, you will need to find out why. Remember to monitor, review and revise your policy, to make sure its stays effective and covers any changes in the workplace, eg buying new equipment.

56 HSE has published detailed guidance on managing health and safety. A selection is listed later in this chapter.

Risk assessment

57 The purpose of risk assessment is to identify what actions you need to take to remove or control the health and safety risks associated with your work – these are known as 'control measures'. Risk assessments also provide a way of measuring your health and safety performance.

58 Risk assessment is an important part of every chapter in this book.

59 HSE has drawn up a simple five-step risk assessment system – see Table 1.

Table 1 Five steps to risk assessment

Step 1	Identify the hazards	You need to think of everything that could cause injuries or other harm in your workplace (a 10-minute walk around the workplace will identify obvious problems and get you started). Feedback from your workers and your accident reports will also help to identify problem areas.
Step 2	Identify who will or could be harmed (injured or made ill)	Include vulnerable people, eg disabled people, young people (16-18 years of age), children, pregnant women and new mothers, and people who may visit your workplace, eg contractors, visitors.
Step 3	Prioritise the associated risks	How likely is the harm to occur and how severe will the harm be if it does occur? For example, a **high** priority risk is a hazard that is very likely to occur and that will cause severe injuries.
Step 4	Identify what actions you need to take to remove or control those risks	These are known as 'control measures'. There is a set of 'prevention principles' (see paragraph 65) that you need to follow when considering control measures; these principles are written down in the Management of Health and Safety at Work Regulations 1999.
Step 5	Review	Review and (if necessary) revise your risk assessments to ensure they stay up to date and take account of any changes in the workplace.

60   If you have five or more employees you must record the significant findings of your risk assessments. It is good practice to record your risk assessments regardless of the number of employees or the level of risk, eg include any low risks identified.

61   Many health and safety regulations require risk assessments to be carried out. However, where specific risk assessments are required, eg for hazardous substances under the Control of Substances Hazardous to Health Regulations 2002 (COSHH), they do not have to be repeated under the general risk assessment requirements in the Management of Health and Safety at Work Regulations 1999.

Hazard
62   A hazard is anything that could (ie, has the potential to) cause harm.

Risk
63   Risk is the likelihood of the hazard occurring and the severity of the harm if it does occur.

Hazard and risk
64   For example, a bottle of bleach with its cap on is a **hazard**, but very little risk. Once you open the bottle and use the bleach, the risk increases, ie there is a risk of spillage, which may cause the bleach to come into contact with your skin. The level of risk will depend on how the bleach is used, who is using it and what protective clothing the user is wearing.

Prevention principles

65   These prevention principles are written in the Management Regulations 1999 and set down the order in which you should think about and apply control measures. Always start at the top of the list and then work your way down to the next step as necessary. The prevention principles are:

■   avoid the risks when ever possible;
■   assess any risks that cannot be avoided;
■   remove or control the risk at its source, eg replace worn or damaged carpet rather than putting out a warning sign;
■   adapt the work to the capabilities of the workers – **never** the other way around;
■   keep up to date and consider using new developments in technology etc;
■   integrate your health and safety control measures into your organisational policies and procedures;
■   where possible, use control measures that protect all the workers who are at risk from a particular hazard (these are known as 'collective' measures) rather than control measures that just protect individuals;
■   provide information, instructions and training to ensure workers understand what they must do and why;
■   develop a positive safety culture within the organisation.

66   In practice, you may have to use a combination of these principles.

Further information

Successful health and safety management HSG65 (Second edition) HSE Books 1997 ISBN 0 7176 1276 7

Management of health and safety at work. Management of Health and Safety at Work Regulations 1999. Approved Code of Practice and guidance L21 (Second edition) HSE Books 2000 ISBN 0 7176 2488 9

Five steps to risk assessment Leaflet INDG163(rev2) HSE Books 2006 (single copy free or priced packs of 10 ISBN 0 7176 6189 X)

Managing health and safety: Five steps to success Leaflet INDG275 HSE Books 1998 (single copy free or priced packs of 10 ISBN 0 7176 2170 7)

Managing contractors: A guide for employers. An open learning booklet HSG159 HSE Books 1997 ISBN 0 7176 1196 5

Information, instruction, supervision and training

67 Providing your workers with the right information, instruction, supervision and training to do their work safely and without risks to their health is a basic requirement of nearly every health and safety law. It should also be one of the control measures identified in each of your risk assessments.

68 Deciding what is needed will depend on a number of factors and will change as new work equipment is bought, new workers are taken on or if there are any changes to the way work is organised. This means you will have to regularly review the information that you give your workers and when necessary, revise it accordingly. It will also depend on the worker's experience. The information that new workers need on their first day will be different to what they need after they have been doing their job for a long time.

69 Like everything else, you need to have a plan for providing information etc. Think about:

- what you want the information, instruction, supervision and/or training to achieve, ie what its purpose is;
- how will you know if you have achieved that what you wanted to? Make sure its effectiveness can be measured;
- how will you review it and identify new needs? Worker appraisals, new equipment purchases, accident reports and risk assessments may give you some indications;
- keeping detailed and dated records of all information, instruction, supervision or training provided to the workers.

Table 2 Health and safety signs

Sign type	Example	Description	Meaning
Prohibition		White circle with red border and cross bar and black picture of activity being prohibited	**Stops** the shown activity where the sign is displayed, eg 'NO SMOKING'
Mandatory		Blue circle with white border and white picture of activity required	Shows when certain actions **must** be taken, eg wearing hard hats, protective gloves etc
Warning		Yellow triangle with black border and black picture of the danger	Identifies the dangers in the area where it is displayed, eg electrical hazards
Safe condition		Green square or rectangle with white writing and/or pictures	Shows the direction of safety or assistance, eg fire exit signs and first-aid kit locations
Fire		Red with white pictures	Identifies location of fire-related equipment, eg fire extinguishers

Getting the message across

70 Any information, instruction or training needs to:

- be simple;
- be relevant;
- be understood by the people it is aimed at – think about:
  - language. Can English be sufficiently understood? Some HSE guidance is available in many languages;
  - format. Can your workers read and write? Written instructions are no good if they can't read;
  - disabilities, eg written instructions are no good for visually impaired workers – you may need spoken or Braille alternatives;
- be possible to follow in the actual workplace;
- allow for feedback from workers;
- be regularly reviewed and if necessary, revised.

Information

71 'Information' is what you tell your workers, either verbally or in writing, to make them aware of the dangers associated with their work and the control measures that they need to follow in order to protect themselves from those dangers. It should also include their health and safety responsibilities and any restrictions or limitations placed on their work, eg prohibiting them using certain machinery if they haven't been trained to use it.

72 An example of providing information is displaying the various health and safety signs around the workplace. The Health and Safety (Safety Signs and Signals) Regulations 1996 define the shapes and colours of these signs depending on what type they are, as shown in Table 2.

Instruction

73 Instructions tell a worker what they can or can't do. For example, instruction manuals explain how a machine or piece of equipment should be used, cleaned or maintained. Again, instructions can be verbal or written.

Supervision

74 Supervision is basically 'keeping an eye on someone' while they work, and is particularly useful in ensuring the health and safety of young or inexperienced workers. It is often carried out by more experienced workers.

Training

75 Training is about giving your workers the skills and knowledge that they need to do their work safely and without risks to their health. Training will be specific to the job and each worker, and must have 'learning outcomes', ie goals that can be measured to ensure the training is effective and relevant. A lot of health and safety training can be incorporated into 'on-the-job' training and does not need workers to be sent away on external courses. The training needs of your workers will change over time and should cover:

- **first day** – fire/first aid, emergency arrangements;
- **induction** – basic awareness of issues such as fire safety, health and safety;
- **work skills** – the skills workers need to do their job, eg moving and handling, safe use of machinery;
- **professional development** – further development of work skills and any professional advancement;
- **refresher training** – to keep work skills up to date and update workers on any technological and/or work changes;
- **compulsory** – approved training that you must provide, eg first-aider training.

76 As voluntary workers should be included in your training programmes, you may need to be flexible with the training times and venues so they can attend. Many volunteers have other jobs or commitments and may not be available Monday-to-Friday, nine-to-five. It may also be worth accepting proof of any health and safety related training that they may have done elsewhere – providing that training covers your own requirements.

Further information

Safety signs and signals. The Health and Safety (Safety Signs and Signals) Regulations 1996. Guidance on Regulations L64 HSE Books 1996 ISBN 0 7176 0870 0

Effective health and safety training: A trainer's resource pack HSG222 HSE Books 2001 ISBN 0 7176 2109 X

Managing health and safety: An open learning workbook for managers and trainers HSE Books 1997 ISBN 0 7176 11531

Signpost to the Health and Safety (Safety Signs and Signals) Regulations 1996 Leaflet INDG184 HSE Books 1996 (single copy free or priced packs of 15 ISBN 0 7176 1139 6)

Figure 1 Information, instruction, supervision and training flow chart

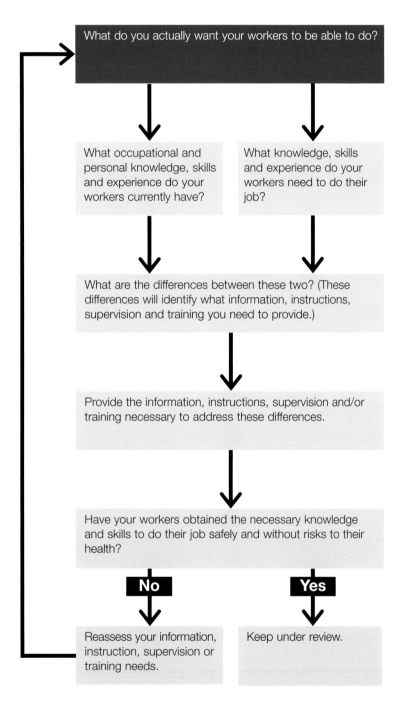

Accidents, sickness and return to work

77 An 'accident' is defined as an unplanned and uncontrolled event at work that has (or could have) resulted in some sort of harm. The harm may be:

- an injury (eg a cut or fracture);
- an illness (eg legionnaires' disease or asbestosis);
- a mental trauma (eg work-related stress or the after effect of a violent attack).

78 While 'health and safety' is all about preventing accidents and ill health occurring, it is important that you are able to collect all the relevant information when they do happen. It is also important that you manage how and when your workers return to work after an accident.

79 This chapter will look at:

- reporting accidents, both within your workplace and to your health and safety enforcing authority (see paragraph 87 about RIDDOR);
- investigating accidents;
- getting workers back to work after an accident.

Reporting accidents

80 Knowing why accidents have happened will help you to stop them happening again. You must therefore have a system for reporting accidents at your workplace so that you are aware of what is actually happening. This system may be your own in-house reporting form or the official HSE accident book.

81 If you don't have a reporting form or accident book, there is a sample CSG accident reporting form in Appendix 3 (from a hospice) that you may use or adapt for your organisation. This form has been approved by the Department for Work and Pensions (DWP).

82 Social security laws also require you to keep a record of all work accidents so that there is supporting information available if an injured worker claims social security benefits as a result of their accident.

What accidents must be reported
83 You need to know about all accidents that occur in your workplace, even if they don't cause any injuries or damage. These are known as near-miss accidents and give you very important information on where you may have more serious accidents at your workplace in the future. They are also the most difficult to find out about so you need to make your

workers aware of the need to report them and to have a simple system for reporting them.

Accident forms/accident book
84 Most employers use an accident report form or the official accident book to report accidents. There is no right or wrong way provided that the necessary information is kept available in some format in case it is needed, eg in a future court case. However you record your accidents, you must make sure that you comply with the data protection requirements on confidentiality to stop any personal information being seen by other people – the new official HSE accident books and CSG accident report form are designed to help you comply with these requirements.

85 DWP is happy to approve in-house accident forms.

86 There are a few simple rules for filling in accident reports:

- use black ink;
- ensure the writing is clear and can be read easily;
- only record facts – don't give opinions;
- include as much information as possible about what happened – use an extra sheet if necessary;
- identify witnesses and record their contact details (in case you need to talk to them later);
- ensure the department manager has to sign the report – this means they will be aware of what is happening in their department and can identify some actions to stop that type of accident happening again;
- if the injured person does not fill in the form, then the name and address of the person who does complete it must be recorded;
- make sure the completed form is returned to a central point where all the accident information from your workplace can be collected and looked at.

RIDDOR

87 You are also required by law to report certain more serious accidents, either directly to your health and safety enforcing authority or centrally to the HSE incident centre. Failure to report these accidents could result in you being taken to court. The law that requires you to report these accidents is the Reporting of Injuries, Diseases and Dangerous Occurrences Regulations 1995 – you will probably know them as RIDDOR.

88 For RIDDOR to apply, the injury, disease or dangerous occurrence must meet one or more of the criteria in paragraph 89 and be associated with your work activities and/or workplace. Serious injuries resulting from acts of violence at work are included.

RIDDOR accidents

89 The following list is a shortened and simplified summary of the main accident criteria that must be reported under RIDDOR. RIDDOR accidents must be associated with a work activity or workplace and include:

- all fatalities;
- specified injuries to people at work, eg:
  - fractures (not to fingers or toes);
  - dislocation of hips, shoulders, knees etc;
  - electric shock or burns;
  - eye injuries;
  - unconsciousness;
- accidents to a person at work that result in the injured person being away from work for more than three days. When reporting 'over-three-day' accidents, remember:
  - you **do not** include the day of the accident in the over-three-day calculation – start with the day after the accident as day one;
  - you **do** include days not normally worked, eg weekends or days off between shifts;
- injury treatment requiring the person at work to stay in hospital for more than 24 hours;
- injuries to any person who is not at work (eg members of the public) that require that person to be immediately taken to hospital for treatment;
- specified occupational diseases caused by:
  - physical agents, eg radiation, vibration;
  - physical demands of the job, eg carpal tunnel syndrome;
  - infections, eg hepatitis, legionellosis;
  - chemicals or substances, eg various cancers, asbestosis;
- specified dangerous occurrences, eg:
  - failure of lifting equipment;
  - failure of a pressure system;
  - gas incidents;
  - structural collapses.

90 The Regulations and guidance give the full list of reportable accidents.

91 The position for reporting RIDDOR accidents involving volunteers is still unclear and volunteers are not included as one of the specified groups under the 'affected person' section on the form. Good practice is therefore to report RIDDOR accidents to volunteers as if they are 'employees' and to specify that they are volunteer workers where the form set up allows.

Reporting RIDDOR accidents

92 There are two main choices for you to report RIDDOR accidents. You may contact your local health and safety enforcing authority (the number should be on your poster *Health and safety law: What you should know*) or you may report them directly to the HSE national Incident Contact Centre (ICC). ICC contact details are given in Appendix 1: *Useful contacts*.

93 You are required to report RIDDOR accidents as soon as they come to your attention. This can be done by:

- telephone;
- fax;
- e-mail;
- via the *Reporting an accident* link on the HSE website (www.hse.gov.uk).

94 If you notify by telephone you must follow your call up with a written report (using form F2508) within 10 days. Notification by e-mail or via the HSE website to ICC generates an automatic written report. A copy of HSE's form F2508 is included in Appendix 3 for you to use.

Investigating accidents

95   If accidents do occur they should be investigated to prevent them from happening again. The main points to consider when investigating accidents that have caused injuries or damage are:

■   ensure that accidents, especially serious ones, are reported immediately;
■   ensure any injured people are safe and given appropriate medical or first-aid treatment;
■   seal off the scene of the accident – this stops other people getting hurt and will save any evidence;
■   record the contact details of any witnesses;
■   take photographs or draw a sketch of the accident scene;
■   take witness statements – this should be in writing and done as soon as possible;
■   find out what caused the accident and why it happened. Don't just look at what caused the injury or damage, find the 'root' cause, ie the first event that occurred in the series of events that led to the injury or damage;
■   decide what you need to do to prevent the same accident happening again, and **do it**;
■   review the actions you have taken to ensure they are effective;
■   make sure your accident form or book is filled in.

Getting workers back to work

96   If any of your workers have been injured or made ill in an accident, including time off for work-related stress, it is important that they are helped to get back to work as quickly as they are able. There is evidence that workers who return to work quickly after an injury or illness absence make a much better recovery, and can save their employer large sums of money in associated costs, eg recruitment, training etc.

97   The key points are:

■   have a policy in your workplace that clearly defines what you will do if your workers have any period of sick leave. What you do will depend on the sick leave period;
■   stay in regular contact with your workers during their absence;
■   give them medical assistance, eg arrange visits to an occupational health service or appropriate therapy sessions (eg physiotherapy etc). This will help to identify if any changes need to be made to the worker's workplace or work arrangements;
■   manage their return to work, eg give them a 'return to work interview', involve them in department meetings or let them return part-time.

Further information

A guide to the Reporting of Injuries, Diseases and Dangerous Occurrences Regulations 1995 L73 (Second edition) HSE Books 1999 ISBN 0 7176 2431 5

RIDDOR explained: Reporting of Injuries, Diseases and Dangerous Occurrences Regulations Leaflet HSE31(rev1) HSE Books 1999 (single copy free or priced packs of 10 ISBN 0 7176 2441 2)

The RIDDOR Incident Contact Centre: Remember! Ring and report! Leaflet MISC310(rev2) HSE Books 2005

Investigating accidents and incidents: A workbook for employers, unions, safety representatives and safety professionals HSG245 HSE Books 2004 ISBN 0 7176 2827 2

Managing sickness absence and return to work: An employer's and manager's guide HSG249 HSE Books 2004 ISBN 0 7176 2882 5

Managing sickness absence and return to work in small businesses Leaflet INDG399 HSE Books 2004 (single copy free or priced packs of 20 ISBN 0 7176 2914 7)

Figure 2 Reporting RIDDOR accidents flow chart

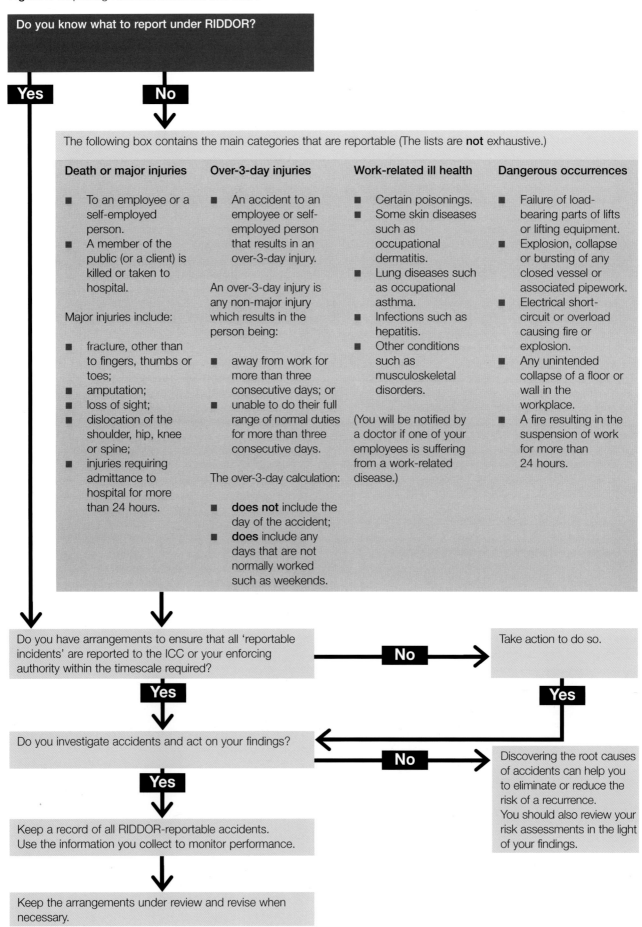

Do you know what to report under RIDDOR?

Yes   **No**

The following box contains the main categories that are reportable (The lists are **not** exhaustive.)

Death or major injuries

- To an employee or a self-employed person.
- A member of the public (or a client) is killed or taken to hospital.

Major injuries include:

- fracture, other than to fingers, thumbs or toes;
- amputation;
- loss of sight;
- dislocation of the shoulder, hip, knee or spine;
- injuries requiring admittance to hospital for more than 24 hours.

Over-3-day injuries

- An accident to an employee or self-employed person that results in an over-3-day injury.

An over-3-day injury is any non-major injury which results in the person being:

- away from work for more than three consecutive days; or
- unable to do their full range of normal duties for more than three consecutive days.

The over-3-day calculation:

- **does not** include the day of the accident;
- **does** include any days that are not normally worked such as weekends.

Work-related ill health

- Certain poisonings.
- Some skin diseases such as occupational dermatitis.
- Lung diseases such as occupational asthma.
- Infections such as hepatitis.
- Other conditions such as musculoskeletal disorders.

(You will be notified by a doctor if one of your employees is suffering from a work-related disease.)

Dangerous occurrences

- Failure of load-bearing parts of lifts or lifting equipment.
- Explosion, collapse or bursting of any closed vessel or associated pipework.
- Electrical short-circuit or overload causing fire or explosion.
- Any unintended collapse of a floor or wall in the workplace.
- A fire resulting in the suspension of work for more than 24 hours.

Do you have arrangements to ensure that all 'reportable incidents' are reported to the ICC or your enforcing authority within the timescale required?   **No** → Take action to do so.

Yes   **Yes**

Do you investigate accidents and act on your findings?   **No** → Discovering the root causes of accidents can help you to eliminate or reduce the risk of a recurrence. You should also review your risk assessments in the light of your findings.

Yes

Keep a record of all RIDDOR-reportable accidents. Use the information you collect to monitor performance.

Keep the arrangements under review and revise when necessary.

Table 3 Management checklist: Reporting accidents and work-related ill health

Checkpoints	Yes, No or N/A	Action required	
		By whom?	By when?
Are there easily understood written arrangements for accident reporting?			
Do the arrangements cover everyone likely to be the victim of work-related accidents or ill health, such as workers, self-employed, contractors, clients and members of the public?			
Do the arrangements cover near misses, injuries, accidents, work-related ill health and dangerous occurrences?			
Do the arrangements cover accidents that may occur away from the employer's premises, such as while travelling for work, at events, in clients' homes, or in the case of homeworkers, while working at home?			
Do the arrangements clearly identify who is responsible for monitoring accident reports and ensuring any reporting required under RIDDOR is done?			
Do the people responsible for submitting RIDDOR reports have access to relevant HSE guidance so they can determine which incidents are reportable?			
Are the people responsible for RIDDOR reporting aware of various ways they can make a report?			
Are all workers made aware of reporting arrangements for near-misses, accidents, work-related ill health, and dangerous occurrences?			
Are accident reporting arrangements included in induction training and is a culture of reporting all incidents encouraged?			
Are workers made aware that all work-related acts of violence against them must be reported?			
Are accident records kept and do they meet the requirements of RIDDOR and the Data Protection Act?			
Do the arrangements identify when it is appropriate to investigate an accident, who should carry out an investigation and what they should be looking for?			
Is the accident and work-related ill health information periodically reviewed to identify trends, common factors and areas where further risk control measures are required?			
Do you check that the arrangements you have established are actually being used and are effective?			

Charity shops

98 Many charity and voluntary organisations have charity shops as part of their fundraising activities. While there are some health and safety issues that are the same as for commercial shops (eg safe displays, customer access and fire safety) there are also some important differences. These differences are:

■ charity shops are often managed solely by volunteers (many only working a few hours a week). This has an impact on worker control, eg training, communication;
■ the shop premises are often on a short-term let or rent agreement. This has implications for premises management issues such as maintenance, asbestos;
■ charity shop stocks generally come from donated goods that are then sold. This means that there is no control over what is actually donated, how much and when.

99 When looking at the health and safety issues, it is useful to divide the shop areas into the rear (non-public) areas and the front display (public) area.

Rear shop area

100 This is where all the donated goods are sorted out, prepared for sale and stored. Common health and safety issues associated with rear shop areas include:

■ lack of working space, leading to poor working postures, an increased likelihood of trips and falls, obstructed fire exit and escape routes;
■ regular moving and handling of heavy bags and boxes;
■ sorting donated goods – possibility of cuts or puncture wounds from hypodermic needles or other sharp objects, contamination from soiled goods (faeces or urine etc), poor posture (prolonged bending over and twisting) often due to working from ground level;
■ high-level storage of items – possibility of items falling on people below;
■ storing items on and/or above heaters;
■ poor environmental conditions, eg little control over lighting, temperature (heating etc) and ventilation;
■ poor premises maintenance and decoration;
■ use and storage of work equipment such as steamers, irons, price-tag guns;
■ use and storage of cleaning equipment and substances;
■ welfare facilities (eg food and drink area, toilets) often in or close to working areas;

■ security – access by the public from within the shop and from outside;
■ vulnerable people, ie older workers and/or work experience students.

Front shop area

101 This is the public area of the shop where customers come in to look at and buy the displayed items. Common health and safety issues associated with the front shop areas are:

■ congested aisles, making access and emergency escapes difficult;
■ slippery floors from wet footwear and drips from umbrellas;
■ loose items left on the floor leading to trips etc;
■ fire – clothing stored or displayed on or above heaters;
■ access to dangerous display items (eg knives, knitting needles), especially by children;
■ contact with display items and/or stands;
■ personal safety, ie dealing with difficult people and possible abuse or violence;
■ access to services by disabled people;
■ access to the till and money;
■ unclear and/or obstructed fire escape routes and fire extinguishers;
■ slippery floors from wet footwear and drips from umbrellas.

Further information

Preventing violence to retail staff HSG133 HSE Books 1995 ISBN 0 7176 0891 3

The Association of Charity Shops (ACS) also produces useful health and safety information, including manager and worker guides and training courses. See Appendix 1: *Useful contacts* for their details.

The Institution of Occupational Safety and Health (IOSH) has a Retail and Distribution Specialist Group that is developing health and safety tools and guidance for the retail and distribution sector – charities are represented.

Case study 1: Sorting donated goods

An elderly volunteer was asked to collect the 20 bags of donated goods left outside the shop after the weekend car-boot sales and to sort the items for storage, disposal or display.

Hazards

- Repetitive moving and handling of a large number of heavy bags.
- Unknown contents – sharp objects, contamination.
- Poor working posture/position – bending over to empty and sort the bags from the floor.
- Work equipment, eg steamer, iron and/or price-tag gun.
- Vulnerable worker – elderly workers may be more susceptible to injury.

Harm

- Back injuries and/or falls on level from moving the bags.
- Cuts or puncture wounds.
- Infections.
- Back, neck, shoulder and upper arm injuries due to bad position and bending and twisting.
- Burns from steam.
- Electric shock.

Solutions

- Share moving and handling between all workers or collect a few bags at a time with a break in between.
- Empty the bags onto a flat surface, preferably a table so all the contents and their condition can be clearly seen before handling.
- Have appropriate protective gloves available, eg for handling sharp objects and to protect against general contamination/soiling.
- Work at table height and plan the position of all other equipment so as to minimise any bending or twisting of the body.
- Use bag openers or holders to keep rag sacks etc open while filling up.
- Allow only authorised use of steaming equipment.
- Ensure ironing board is height adjustable.
- Planned preventative maintenance, eg portable appliance testing (PAT) on all electrical equipment.

Case study 2: High-level storage

An elderly volunteer used a chair to reach some bric-a-brac objects stored on a high shelf.

Hazards

- Work at height.
- Poor posture – reaching/stretching.
- Moving and handling.
- Chair – unstable and unsuitable, ie not used for its intended use.
- Age of worker and worker's abilities.
- Falling objects – possibly sharp.

Harm

- Injuries from falls.
- Back and upper limb injuries.
- Cuts.
- Injury risks to people nearby.

Solutions

- Organise storage to avoid potentially dangerous items on high shelves.
- Avoid working at height, eg use long-handled grips to reach high items.
- Use appropriate equipment, eg stepladder with a supporting handrail.
- Visual checks on stepladder before use to confirm it is not defective.
- Planned equipment maintenance.
- Consider physical limitations of worker, eg mobility and medical conditions such as vertigo or low blood pressure.

Notes

1   Many charity shops provide 'kick stools' for workers to stand on to reach higher level items – if you provide these you need to think of the people using them, ie older people will find it difficult to step up onto them and will feel unstable once up without any supporting handholds.

Case study 3: Steamer

A new shop employee used a steamer to prepare donated clothing for display and sale.

Hazards
■ Hot water.
■ Electricity.
■ Poor working posture.
■ Trailing wires and hose.

Harm
■ Burns/scalds.
■ Electric shock/electrocution – electricity and water.
■ Back and upper limb injuries.
■ Trips.

Solutions
■ Induction training and instruction in what workers can and can't do.
■ Training and instruction to ensure competent use of equipment.
■ Restricted use of equipment until the worker is competent.
■ Visual checks before use, equipment maintenance, PAT testing – keep records.

Case study 4: Safe sorting

A volunteer at a charity shop was sorting through a bag of donated clothing when they jabbed themselves on a used hypodermic needle that was mixed up with the clothing.

Hazards
■ Needle-stick injury, needle from unknown source.
■ Unknown weight and contents – bag of donations could include items that are soiled or with sharp or broken edges.

Harm
■ Contract infection/disease via puncture wound, eg HIV and hepatitis.
■ Stress and anxiety while awaiting blood test results.
■ Cuts from sharp or broken objects.
■ Back injury from lifting heavy bag.
■ Back injury from stooping to empty bag.

Solutions
■ Use sack trolley to move heavy sacks of donations.
■ Empty contents of bag onto waist-high sorting table and visually inspect donations.
■ Wear heavy-duty gloves for initial sorting and for removing any broken crockery etc.
■ Train all sorters to use a safe sorting technique.

Case study 5: Unsafe storage area

A charity shop had recently received a large volume of donations and the backroom storage area was full. It was decided to store the excess donations in the cellar, which was reached by a steep wooden ladder via a hatch in the sales area.

Hazards
■ Unsafe access – ladder with no handrail.
■ Manual handling – carrying donations down ladder.
■ Unsuitable storage area – low ceiling, poor lighting, no shelving, damp.
■ Someone could fall into cellar when hatch open.

Harm
■ Serious multiple injuries, possibly fatal, if fall into cellar or slip off ladder.
■ Injuries from slipping or tripping in cellar due to poor lighting, damp environment and stock on floor.
■ Head injury if strike against ceiling beams.
■ Back injury from moving goods in restricted area.

Solutions
■ Fully review stock flow and management at shop – consider where stock is obtained from, quality of donations and quality of stock being stored.
■ Redesign backroom layout to fully utilise space available.
■ Increase number of people working on sorting incoming donations.
■ Increase frequency of waste collections.
■ Rent additional storage space locally.
■ Hire van to transport good quality donations to other shops in your network.
■ Instruct staff to refuse donations if no storage space available.

Notes
1   The local environmental health department served a prohibition notice on the use of this cellar for storage purposes.

Case study 6: Emptying textile bank

As part of a local recycling area, a charity retailer had a textile bank sited in a supermarket car park for receipt of donations. The shop manager of the local branch of the charity visited the bank on a weekly basis to empty the contents. The manager used their own car to transport the contents back to their shop for sorting.

Hazards
- Personal security/lone working – bank located in dark area of car park.
- Traffic movement.
- Manual handling – bending, stooping and moving heavy loads into car.
- Slips and trips – debris around recycling area.
- Unknown contents – bank could contain rubbish or soiled items, including used needles, broken glass etc.
- Sharp edges on metal bank.

Harm
- Multiple injuries if hit by car.
- Contract infection/disease via cuts or puncture wound, eg HIV and hepatitis. Stress and anxiety while awaiting blood test results.
- Cuts and bruises from sharp edges of bank or broken objects inside.
- Back injury from transporting heavy items to car.
- Back injury from stooping to access inside bank.

Solutions
- Empty bank in daylight hours, when supermarket is open.
- Carry mobile phone and notify responsible person where you are going and what time you expect to return to the shop.
- Park as close to the bank as possible to minimise carrying distance.
- Wear heavy-duty gloves.
- Provide a torch so the inside and contents of the bank are clearly visible and inspect items before picking them up.
- Provide empty bags or boxes so contents of bank can be transferred into loads of manageable size and weight.
- Use separate boxes for rubbish or sharp items.
- Maintenance of banks – introduce routine maintenance/replacement/fault reporting system.
- Monitor volume and quality of donations from bank, vandalism and debris deposited inside. Consider relocating bank if necessary.

Notes
1   Individuals who use their private cars for collecting donations should be insured for business use.
2   There have been several fatalities from people getting trapped inside textile banks.

Case study 7: Slips, trips and falls

While shopping in a charity shop, an elderly customer, who walked with the aid of a walking stick, tripped and fell over a toy lorry that was on the sales floor, partially under some display shelving. Earlier in the day, a young child had taken the toy off the display shelf and had been playing with it on the floor. The customer was taken to hospital by ambulance.

Hazards
- Tripping – obstacles on floor.
- Vulnerable individual.

Harm
- Fractured hip – the individual had a long recovery period and now lacks the confidence to go out on their own and has felt the need to apply for sheltered accommodation.
- Incident reportable under RIDDOR – investigation by local EHO.
- Many of the shop team knew the individual and felt guilty about the incident.

Solutions
- Two members of the shop team are now on duty in the sales area at all times – one of them is continuously monitoring the sales area for items on the floor or stock that looks unsafely displayed.
- Toys are no longer displayed on the two lower shelves, so they cannot be reached by children in pushchairs or by toddlers.

Case study 8: Use of a pricing gun

A new volunteer in a charity shop was asked to price up a rail of clothing that had already been sorted and then take the items out to the sales area and hang them up. The new volunteer was told to watch herself on the gun and keep her fingers out the way. The volunteer was careful when using the gun and suffered no injuries. When she had finished pricing she put it down on the workbench and took the clothing to the sales floor. Another volunteer working in the back room area knocked the gun off the workbench. The needle punctured the lower part of her leg as it fell.

Hazards
- Sharp point on pricing gun.

Harm
- Puncture wounds from pricing gun leading to infected wound.

Solutions
- Full training on the safe use and storage of pricing guns to be given.
- When not in use, the needle must be covered by the needle guard or cap.
- Guns to be stored safely.
- Needles to be replaced or sterilised if they draw blood.
- Safe system for replacing needles and their safe disposal.

Figure 3 Charity shops flow chart

Have you identified everything in your shop that could harm someone?

Yes   **No**

Do (or could) any of the following factors apply to your shop? (The lists are **not** exhaustive.)

General	Front area	Backrooms	Environment
■ Slip and trip hazards. ■ Lifting, carrying and moving items. ■ Obstructed stairs, walkways, and emergency routes. ■ Portable heaters. ■ Equipment, eg pricing guns, stepladders etc. ■ Working alone. ■ Young, elderly and vulnerable workers. ■ Contractor/ maintenance work. ■ Lack of emergency arrangements (fire, first aid etc). ■ No accident book or reporting procedure.	■ Overloaded and/or unstable shop fittings. ■ Items stored or displayed above head height. ■ Displays that are not child-friendly. ■ Handling money. ■ Dealing with difficult people. ■ Obstructed walkways and exits. ■ Unsuitable and/or unmarked glazing in entrance doors and shop windows.	■ Sorting donated goods from floor. ■ Inadequate/ unsecured shelving and racking. ■ Use of steamers and/or electrical appliances. ■ Clutter/excess stock. ■ Locked/blocked fire exits. ■ Chemicals (eg for cleaning). ■ Obstructed fire extinguishers. ■ Use of cellars and attics for storage. ■ Covered heaters.	■ Restricted work space. ■ Poor lighting. ■ Temperature excessively hot/cold. ■ Poor ventilation. ■ Unsafe electrical installations. ■ Unmaintained gas appliances. ■ Waste accumulation. ■ Poor cleanliness and hygiene standards. ■ Inadequate welfare provisions (toilets, hand washing facilities, drinking water etc).

For each factor, have you determined:

■ Who could be harmed?
■ How could the harm occur?
■ What the likely severity of the harm could be?

No → Take action to do so.

Yes

Have you taken sufficient precautions to prevent harm and to comply with your legal duties?

No → The risk of someone being harmed by your activities is **unacceptable.**

Obtain further advice or assistance.

Yes

Record your findings.

Keep the situation under review and revise your precautions when necessary.

Table 4 Management checklist: Charity shops

Checkpoints	Yes, No or N/A	Action required	
		By whom?	By when?
Is the poster *Health and safety law: What you should know* completed and on display?			
Is your safety policy up to date and have you explained it to your workers?			
Does your shop meet basic workplace standards (eg for lighting, temperature, ventilation, doors, stairs, floors, windows, cleanliness, toilet and washing facilities)?			
Are your racking, shelving and display units strong enough for the loads they need to carry and are they stable/securely fixed?			
Have you carried out the necessary risk assessments and recorded the significant findings? (See chapter *Managing health and safety and risk assessment*.)			
In particular, have you assessed the risks associated with: ■ lifting and carrying activities (see chapter *Moving and handling*); ■ sorting of donated goods; ■ storage and display of retail items; ■ slip and trip hazards (such as slippery floors, torn carpets, trailing cables, poorly marked steps, obstructed walkways and stairs, cluttered backrooms, storage and retail areas); ■ fire (see chapter *Fire safety*); ■ equipment, including electrical appliances (see chapter *Work equipment*); ■ ladders and stepladders; ■ maintenance work; ■ work-related violence (see chapter *Violence at work*); ■ cash handling; ■ substances and chemicals (eg cleaning chemicals – see chapter *Hazardous substances*); ■ sharps; ■ goods/passenger lift?			
Have you identified any workers who may be particularly at risk (eg because of their age, lack of experience, a medical condition, an impairment or because they are a new or expectant mother)?			
Have you considered the risks to your customers (including young children and the elderly)?			
Have you put the necessary precautions and procedures in place to control all the risks you have identified?			
Do you have effective arrangements for managing the activities of any contractors?			
Have you provided your workers with sufficient information, instruction and training so they can carry out their work safely? (See chapter *Information, instruction, supervision and training*.)			
Is health and safety included in the induction of all new workers?			
Do your workers know what action to take in an emergency, such as a fire or accident?			

Table 4 Management checklist: Charity shops (continued)

Checkpoints	Yes, No or N/A	Action required	
		By whom?	By when?
Is there a first-aid kit in the shop and does someone have responsibility for looking after it?			
Do you have an accident book? Does everyone in the shop know where it is kept and what to record in it?			
Do you have suitable arrangements in place for RIDDOR accidents? (See chapter *Accidents, sickness absence and returning to work*.)			
Do you check that the precautions you have established are actually being used and are effective?			

Driving and transport

102 UK road safety is controlled by road traffic laws enforced by the police, but some aspects of driving and vehicles are subject to health and safety laws. Many work activities require use of vehicles off road, eg in warehouses, grounds maintenance, environmental projects and overseas.

103 Relevant health and safety issues to consider are:

- policies and procedures for driving at work;
- worker use of the organisation's vehicles;
- use of personal vehicles for work purposes;
- transporting patients or clients in personal or organisation vehicles;
- minibuses;
- people and vehicles in close proximity, eg at fundraising events;
- use of fork-lift trucks, eg in warehouses;
- large goods vehicles (LGVs) used in distribution;
- use of vehicles overseas;
- agricultural and/or all-terrain vehicles (ATVs) in farming, conservation, forestry and similar activities.

104 The main points to consider in your driving policies and risk assessments are:

- drivers;
- passengers;
- vehicles;
- driving conditions;
- work activities.

105 In many cases, drivers will be lone workers, so effective contact arrangements need to be in place and appropriate first-aid equipment provided (eg small travel first-aid kits).

Drivers

106 There are several factors you need to consider when deciding if a driver is competent and safe to drive including:

- awareness of the organisation's driving at work policies and procedures;
- the driver's medical fitness to drive;
- the driver's age. While age in itself is not a problem, youth and inexperience or the effects of normal ageing may make some people unsafe to drive;
- driver experience and training. These are particularly relevant for specialist vehicles, eg fork-lift trucks (drivers must do specialist training and be certificated), LGVs, minibuses;

- appropriate driving licences for the type of vehicle to be driven – there should be procedures to check these and any penalty points accumulated;
- current driving insurance.

Passengers

107 The main points to consider regarding passengers are:

- proper restraints, eg seatbelts, car seats and wheelchair clamps;
- escorts;
- passenger numbers and behaviour;
- special equipment, eg oxygen cylinders or guide dogs;
- plans for rescue and transport in the event of vehicle breakdown.

Vehicles

108 Similarly, there are several points to consider regarding vehicles, including:

- roadworthiness, eg current vehicle MOT (if the vehicle is over three years old). You will need to confirm this information for any personal vehicles used for work activities as well as for the organisation's own vehicles;
- procedures for carrying out regular vehicle checks before each journey, eg check lights, wipers, brakes, fuel. Procedures for reporting faults should be included;
- appropriate insurances;
- breakdown cover (this may be important for lone workers on call overnight or workers who transport passengers);
- vehicle suitability for the intended use and driver's ability and skills.

Driving conditions

109 Your drivers should be prepared for the conditions they are likely to be driving in. These include adverse weather and city/town driving.

110 Weather conditions that need special attention are:

- snow/ice – carry blankets, hot drinks, shovels etc;
- fog;
- very hot weather – carry plenty of liquids to prevent dehydration;
- heavy rain.

111 If the weather conditions are bad, only essential work activities should be carried out. These essential work activities should be planned to take account of the weather conditions and where necessary extra time and/or different routes should be allowed.

112 Urban conditions that need special attention are:

■ congestion and traffic charging schemes;
■ street crime issues, eg carjacking, theft from vehicles while stationary at junctions.

Mobile phones

113 It is illegal to use a non-hands-free mobile phone while driving. The organisation's policies should ideally prohibit the use of any mobile phones while driving and ensure work arrangements are in place to prevent drivers being called or having to make calls. Acceptable 'hands-free' phones are available, but their use is not recommended.

Work arrangements

114 Work activities involving driving, vehicle use or people and vehicles in close proximity (eg fundraising events and car parks) must be identified and assessed. Procedures for removing or reducing associated health and safety risks must be drawn up. These may include:

■ prohibiting use of mobile phones while driving – this may be a complete ban or may allow for 'hands-free' use;
■ ensure drivers only drive for up to two hours before taking a rest break – this will help prevent driving fatigue and allow a change in body posture/position, so preventing back aches etc;
■ allowing for route and/or appointment changes to meet current driving conditions;
■ identifying specialist driving that may require special training, licenses and/or skills, eg fork-lift trucks, LGVs, ATVs, towing trailers or caravans;
■ clear guidance on dealing with and reporting vehicle accidents.

115 Work arrangements and schedules should be agreed so as not to put pressure on workers to answer mobile phones or miss driving breaks etc.

Traffic routes and sites

116 Many work-related traffic accidents occur where vehicles and pedestrians are in the same place at the same time, such as vehicle loading/unloading bays, roads on site, car parks and garages. When keeping people and vehicles apart, consider:

■ procedures and information to warn workers of the associated dangers and any restrictions in place;
■ clear, well-marked traffic and/or pedestrian routes;
■ well lit areas;
■ warning signals when vehicles reverse;
■ the need to control/supervise or stop pedestrian access to vehicle areas at busy times;
■ providing high-visibility jackets for workers in high-risk areas.

Further information

Driving at work: Managing work-related road safety Leaflet INDG382 HSE Books 2003 (single copy free or priced packs of 4 ISBN 0 7176 2740 3)

Reducing at-work road traffic incidents HSE Books 2001 ISBN 0 7176 2239 8

Workplace transport safety: An employers' guide HSG136 (Second edition) HSE Books 2005 ISBN 0 7176 6154 7

Workplace transport safety: An overview Leaflet INDG199(rev1) HSE Books 2005 (single copy free or priced packs of 5 ISBN 0 7176 2821 3)

Health and safety in road haulage Leaflet INDG379 HSE Books 2003 (single copy free or priced packs of 15 ISBN 0 7176 2765 9)

Case study 9: Vehicle used for making collections

A member of staff makes regular collections of donated items for a charity shop, delivering these to a sorting point. The vehicle is a large transit-type van; collections can take five to six hours a day and involve long periods of driving.

Hazards
- Vehicle, eg not roadworthy or unsuitable for activity.
- Adverse driving conditions.
- Driver capability and skills, eg tiredness, experience with type of vehicle.
- Frequent moving and handling of large and heavy items.
- Large quantity of loose items in the vehicle.

Harm
- Increased risk of a road accident.
- Back injury, eg from moving and handling and long periods of driving.
- Injury from movement of loose items stored in the vehicle.

Solutions
- Routine vehicle checks before use and a planned maintenance programme.
- Be prepared for likely driving conditions.
- Ensure the driver is suitably trained for vehicle, activity and conditions.
- Agree the route and the provision of breaks, and ensure these are taken.
- Rearrange collection routes to reduce the length of driving if possible.
- Agree a policy on the size and weight of items that can be collected by one person.
- Provide shelving or means to secure the items stored in the van.

Case study 10: Transporting patients in personal vehicles

Volunteer drivers use their own vehicles to transport patients to and from a medical centre. (The hazards, harm and solutions associated with vehicle roadworthiness, driving conditions and driver capabilities etc are the same as for Case study 9.)

Hazards
- Transferring patients.
- Transferring medical equipment.
- Fire (particularly if oxygen cylinders are being carried).

Harm
- Medical emergencies.
- Injuries from equipment being carried.
- Injuries from road traffic accidents.
- Fire damage and loss.

Solutions
- Avoid use of personal vehicles whenever possible.
- Organisation to provide or arrange suitable vehicles for patients' needs.
- Where the patient has been assessed as requiring medical assistance, a suitable escort should be provided – this may be a first aider or professional nurse.
- Vehicle recovery arrangements need to include onwards assistance for any patients being transported.
- Procedures detailing acceptable driving behaviour, including in emergencies.
- Procedures in place for managing a medical emergency, eg emergency pack, contact numbers and a means of communication kept in the vehicle.
- Safe and secure means for transporting associated medical equipment, eg oxygen cylinders, wheelchairs.

Notes
1 The patients may have complex medical needs which would influence the level of risk and required competence of the driver. Drivers must be 'supernumerary' (ie not included or involved in the care of patients).
2 Drivers are legally responsible for their vehicles (even if they are driving their charity's vehicles), their own safety and that of any passengers.

Case study 11: Temporary storage and distribution premises

A charity hires old warehouse premises to co-ordinate, stockpile and then transport boxes of emergency aid.

Hazards
- Unsuitable premises.
- Vehicle and pedestrian movements in same areas.
- Large vehicles reversing.

Harm
- Death or serious injury caused by contact with vehicles.
- Property and/or vehicle damage.

Solutions
- Clearly define pedestrian and vehicle routes – ideally away from each other.
- If pedestrians have to cross vehicle routes, provide clearly marked areas where they can do this, eg well lit and clearly marked zebra crossings.
- Ensure vehicle areas are well lit and kept unobstructed.
- Ensure all vehicles have a working reversing warning sound and reversing lights to warn pedestrians.
- Prohibit or organise work to minimise pedestrian access when the vehicles are busiest.
- Define set times for vehicle deliveries and collections.
- Provide all workers in the vehicle and loading areas with high-visibility coats/jackets.

Figure 4 Driving and transport flow chart

If the work activity involves driving, have you assessed and removed or controlled the associated risks?

Yes

No

Consider any of the following that could apply. (The lists are **not** exhaustive.)

Drivers

- Fitness to drive, eg age, medical conditions.
- Experience.
- Specialist skills and training, eg HGV, fork-lift trucks, ATVs.
- Appropriate and clean driving licence.
- Appropriate insurance for work use.

Traffic routes

- Well marked.
- Well lit.
- Area used for planned work.
- High-visibility jackets worn.

Passengers

- Proper restraints available and used.
- Escorts – suitable number and experience for passengers.
- Passenger numbers.
- Likely or possible behaviour of passengers.
- Specialist equipment with passengers, eg oxygen cylinders.
- Emergency rescue plans.

Vehicles

- Clear procedure for personal and organisation vehicle use.
- Suitable for intended use.
- In safe road condition, eg current MOT.
- Procedures for carrying out vehicle checks – before every use, checks and planned maintenance.
- Appropriate insurances.
- Breakdown cover and rescue plans.

Conditions

Weather:

- snow/ice;
- very hot;
- fog;
- heavy rain;
- essential journeys only.

Urban:

- traffic congestion;
- road charges, eg toll roads and bridges, congestion charges;
- known and likely street crime types and areas.

Arrangements

- Specialist skills or training required, eg HGVs, fork-lift trucks, ATVs.
- Prohibiting mobile phone use or allow hands-free use only.
- Regular rest breaks during long periods of driving.
- Adjustments to schedules and routes.
- Guidance on dealing with and reporting road accidents.

Take action to do so. ← **Yes** ← Can you do anything about them?

No

Keep under review and revise as necessary.

Risks may be **unacceptable** – consider getting extra help.

Table 5 Management checklist: Driving and transport

Checkpoints	Yes, No or N/A	Action required	
		By whom?	By when?
Driver			
Is the driver medically fit and legally qualified to drive the vehicle? ■ Current driving licence? ■ Any medical conditions to take into account? ■ Appropriate insurances? ■ Experienced in the work? ■ Informed not to use mobile phones while driving?			
Vehicle			
Is the vehicle in good condition and suitable for its intended use? ■ If more than three years old, is there a current MOT? ■ Is there a current insurance certificate? (Note: If private vehicles are used for business, the above would all still be relevant and you would need to check that the insurance covered business use.) ■ Is there breakdown cover? (Particularly important if transporting passengers.)			
Is there a system for routine vehicle safety checks before use? ■ Petrol and oil levels? ■ Water levels? ■ Windscreen wipers? ■ Clean windows and mirrors? ■ Brakes working? ■ Indicators working? ■ Tyres fully inflated and in good condition? ■ Use of seatbelts. Are restraints confirmed before starting the engine?			
Passengers			
Are escorts required?			
Are seat belts in good condition?			
Are workers trained in safe use of restraints, eg wheelchair clamps, tailgate lifts?			
Are there any special needs to be considered?			

Table 5 Management checklist: Driving and transport (continued)

Checkpoints	Yes, No or N/A	Action required	
		By whom?	By when?
Planning and emergency procedures			
Has the journey been planned to include rest breaks if necessary?			
Has the route been planned?			
Have traffic and weather conditions been considered?			
Is the first-aid equipment adequate?			
Is any special equipment (eg oxygen cylinders) properly secured?			
Is there a rescue plan in the event of breakdown or accident, with a means of communication, eg mobile phone?			
Traffic routes			
Are work activities organised to avoid people and vehicles coming together?			
Are vehicle and pedestrian routes clearly marked?			
Are areas well lit?			
Are high-visibility jackets provided?			

Fire safety

117 Fire safety is covered in this book as it is often included under the organisation's health and safety responsibilities and is an important part of ensuring workers' safety. Fire safety has its own set of laws, which will be updated and replaced by the Regulatory Reform (Fire Safety) Order 2005 and the Fire (Scotland) Act 2005 when they come into force. Fire legislation is enforced by local fire authorities.

118 Fire safety is based on the same principles of risk assessment, ie to identify fire hazards and any actions necessary to remove or control those hazards.

119 You need to have a fire safety management system in place that covers all aspects of fire safety in your workplace.

Fire safety management system

120 Your fire safety management system should include:

- fire policy for the workplace, eg fire responsibilities, evacuation procedures etc;
- fire risk assessment – follow HSE's 'five step' guide, but in particular:
  - identify where all the heat and ignition sources are in your workplace;
  - identify where all the flammable and combustible materials are in your workplace;
  where these two factors are present in the same place is where you have the greatest fire risk:
  - identify any vulnerable people, ie people with mobility and/or sensory disabilities (eg people in wheelchairs, people with visual or hearing impairments);
  - think about contractors working on site – what equipment and substances are they using and storing in your workplace;
- training programme and records:
  - fire evacuation procedures and responsibilities – on a worker's first day of work;
  - fire evacuation drills;
  - basic fire safety training;
- premises information:
  - plans of the workplace showing location of high fire risk areas, eg boiler houses, kitchens, laundries;
  - clearly marked fire escape routes and exits;
  - location of any hazardous materials in the workplace, eg asbestos;
  - location of flammable and/or combustible material stores;
  - other relevant information, eg presence of medical oxygen (cylinders or piped);
- emergency procedures for dealing with:
  - contractors on site;
  - firefighter strikes;
  - unexpected changes to the normal fire procedures, eg fire alarm faults or servicing.

Further information

Detailed guidance to accompany the Regulatory Reform (Fire Safety) Order 2005 and the Fire (Scotland) Act 2005 is currently being produced by the Office of the Deputy Prime Minister.

Case study 12: Use of candles

A resident with physical disabilities in a registered care home requested that scented candles were lit each evening on retiring to bed.

Hazards
- Increased risk of fire.

Outcomes
- Loss of life and property.

Solutions
- Discuss if there are alternatives such as a coloured light and separate fragrances.
- Agree the basis on which the candles can be used.
- Location of the candles – away from any combustible materials.
- Position – held securely in candle holders or lanterns.
- Period when alight – how long will the candle be lit, who will be responsible for ensuring it is put out and safe.

Notes
1   Insurers increasingly expect high-risk activities that place life and property at increased risk are managed by risk assessment and may need to be reported to ensure the cover is maintained.

Case study 13: Arson

A remote outbuilding is used to store various substances (including solvents, gas cylinders and other flammable substances) and equipment used by the park maintenance department. The outbuilding is surrounded by piles of logs and general debris. There have been reports of fires in the vicinity that are believed to have been due to arson.

Hazards
- Presence of combustible and flammable items and substances.
- Remoteness of building – ineffective security.
- Easy access to combustible items outside, eg logs.

Harm
- Injuries (possibly death) and property damage due to fire and/or smoke.
- Loss of working materials.
- Replacement costs.
- Increased insurance premiums and/or reduced insurance cover.
- Potential liability claims from other parties.

Solutions
- Include this outbuilding in your fire safety management plan.
- Carry out a risk assessment for the outbuilding and its contents.
- Store logs and other combustible items well away from the building and any public access points.
- Ensure building is lockable and secure.
- Provide a lockable, fire-resistant cupboard or store for all the flammable substances.
- Keep minimum quantities of substances and materials in the outbuilding.
- Increase security and lighting in the area.
- Fit a smoke alarm to warn workers of fire while they are working there.
- Provide appropriate fire extinguishers in the outbuilding – train workers to use them.
- Organise regular collection of logs to avoid stockpiles building up around the area.
- Ensure the area is kept clean and tidy.

Notes
1   Insurers expect to be informed of high-risk activities and situations to ensure the level of cover is sufficient.

Case study 14: Emergency evacuation

A meeting of valued supporters was being organised at an external venue. A number of the supporters were known to be elderly with various mobility impairments. The meeting was arranged in a room on the second floor of the building. However, it was discovered that the venue didn't have any evacuation arrangements for people who couldn't get out without help. The meeting organiser only thought to check this with the venue shortly before the meeting because of publicity surrounding the fire service strikes that were happening at the time. The meeting had to be hastily rearranged at additional cost and inconvenience.

Hazards
- Entrapment in the building due to inappropriate emergency evacuation routes and procedures.

Harm
- Serious injuries or death.
- Bad publicity.

Solutions
- Make arrangements to address any special needs of the people attending the event.
- Choose a suitable venue.
- Visit and check out the venue before confirming booking.
- Get a copy of the venue's fire evacuation procedures and confirm any changes necessary to meet the needs of people attending.
- Review and (if necessary) revise all fire arrangements in exceptional cases, eg firefighter strikes.

Notes
1   If specialised equipment is available to help in emergency evacuations (eg 'evac-u-chairs' used for evacuating wheelchair users down stairs) make sure that someone who has been trained to use it is going to be present.

Case study 15: Contact with light bulb

A large pile of paper files with some complementary therapy equipment on top were left on a work surface underneath a set of wall cupboards. The lights in the bottom of the wall cupboards were left on at the end of the day. When the cleaner came in the following morning, there was a strong smell of burning and the equipment headrest had a large burn mark on its surface.

Hazards
- Combustible items in contact with a very hot object.

Harm
- Fire.
- Property damage.

Solutions
- Keep combustible items and heat sources apart.
- Ensure all therapy equipment is fire retardant.
- Carry out end-of-day checks to ensure all lights and electrical items are turned off.
- File away all paperwork at the end of the day.

Notes
1   There is sufficient heat in light bulbs to set flammable or combustible items alight if they are in contact for a long enough period; wooden furniture pushed up against light fittings can catch fire.
2   This situation often arises in store cupboards; they often have bare bulbs, are used to store combustible items, are left unattended for long periods and are not covered by fire alarm systems.

Case study 16: Second-hand furniture

A furniture recycling project collects and delivers used household furniture. This is then stored in and sold from a warehouse.

Hazards
- Combustible items, eg furniture.
- Presence of any heat or ignition sources.
- Furniture that does not comply with current standards and laws, eg fire retardancy requirements.
- Moving and handling activities – heavy, bulky and awkward loads.

Harm
- Injuries (possibly death) and property damage due to fire and/or smoke.
- Unknown future viability of the project.
- Injuries due to moving and handling furniture.
- Potential liability for safety of furniture purchased.

Solutions
- Keep items of furniture away from any heat or ignition sources.
- Register the property with the local authority.
- Notify the local fire authority and liaise on the necessary fire safety arrangements, eg fire risk assessment.
- Ensure there is a detailed fire safety management system in place.
- Ensure the fire risk assessment is valid and regularly reviewed.
- Train all workers in line with the fire risk assessment and fire evacuation procedure.
- Carry out training for workers on selecting and moving suitable items to be collected – specialist 'furniture moving' training should be considered.
- Organise storage in the warehouse to minimise fire and moving and handling risks.
- Provide moving and handling aids to reduce the moving and handling tasks.

Notes
1   It is the duty of the person who controls the premises to carry out a fire risk assessment. Where more than one organisation is involved on a site there is an absolute duty to co-operate in ensuring the assessment is adequate and everyone involved knows their responsibilities.

Figure 5 Fire safety flow chart

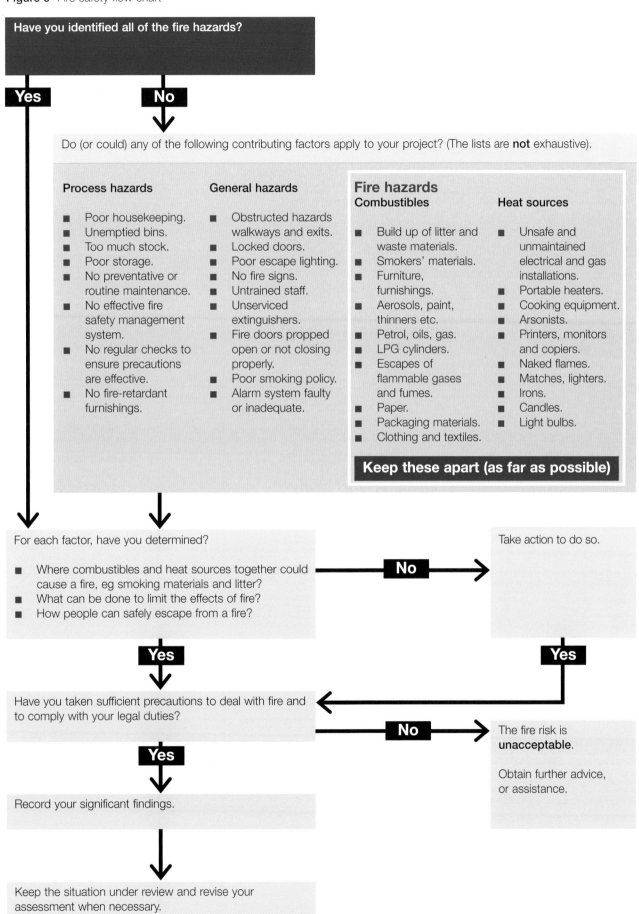

Have you identified all of the fire hazards?

Yes　　**No**

Do (or could) any of the following contributing factors apply to your project? (The lists are **not** exhaustive).

Process hazards

- Poor housekeeping.
- Unemptied bins.
- Too much stock.
- Poor storage.
- No preventative or routine maintenance.
- No effective fire safety management system.
- No regular checks to ensure precautions are effective.
- No fire-retardant furnishings.

General hazards

- Obstructed hazards walkways and exits.
- Locked doors.
- Poor escape lighting.
- No fire signs.
- Untrained staff.
- Unserviced extinguishers.
- Fire doors propped open or not closing properly.
- Poor smoking policy.
- Alarm system faulty or inadequate.

Fire hazards

Combustibles

- Build up of litter and waste materials.
- Smokers' materials.
- Furniture, furnishings.
- Aerosols, paint, thinners etc.
- Petrol, oils, gas.
- LPG cylinders.
- Escapes of flammable gases and fumes.
- Paper.
- Packaging materials.
- Clothing and textiles.

Heat sources

- Unsafe and unmaintained electrical and gas installations.
- Portable heaters.
- Cooking equipment.
- Arsonists.
- Printers, monitors and copiers.
- Naked flames.
- Matches, lighters.
- Irons.
- Candles.
- Light bulbs.

Keep these apart (as far as possible)

For each factor, have you determined?

- Where combustibles and heat sources together could cause a fire, eg smoking materials and litter?
- What can be done to limit the effects of fire?
- How people can safely escape from a fire?

No →

Take action to do so.

Yes　　**Yes**

Have you taken sufficient precautions to deal with fire and to comply with your legal duties?

No →

The fire risk is **unacceptable**.

Obtain further advice, or assistance.

Yes

Record your significant findings.

Keep the situation under review and revise your assessment when necessary.

Table 6 Management checklist: Fire safety

Checkpoints	Yes, No or N/A	Action required	
		By whom?	By when?
Are signs displayed showing what to do in the event of a fire?			
Are workers trained so that they behave appropriately in the event of a fire?			
Do people know your policy on tackling fires? Have they been trained and know not to be a hero?			
Are there systems in place to maintain, check and record the effectiveness and serviceability of: ■ the fire alarm system, including break-glass points, smoke/heat detectors, smoke alarms, sounders; ■ emergency/escape lighting; ■ fire-fighting equipment; ■ fire doors; ■ door closers; ■ panic bars and lock-release mechanisms on exit doors; ■ smoke seals; ■ intumescent (heat expanding) strips; ■ fire signs.			
Are systems in place to ensure that fire escapes (including routes outside the final exit) are kept clear and are external fire stairs slip free and safe?			
Where a fire alarm system is installed, is there a plan of the building adjacent to the main panel showing fire zones?			
Are there any special requirements for disabled staff and volunteers, eg visual or vibrating alerting devices for the deaf?			
Are non-essential electrical appliances switched off and unplugged when not in use?			
Has the fixed electrical wiring been tested and inspected in the last five to ten years?			
Are portable appliances regularly inspected and tested by a competent person, eg are the PAT tests up to date?			
Do users of electrical equipment know that they have a responsibility for visual checks, eg making sure that cord grips are tight, no exposed wires, no overheating, no frayed flexes?			
Do you have a policy that prohibits staff and volunteers bringing unsafe electrical appliances into the workplace?			
Is there a smoking policy in place that is adequate to reduce the likelihood of accidents with smoking materials?			
Are metal bins provided for disposing of cigarettes etc?			
Is waste material cleared frequently and are housekeeping procedures adequate?			
Are stock levels maintained to reduce the presence of flammable material?			

Table 6 Management checklist: Fire safety (continued)

Checkpoints	Yes, No or N/A	Action required	
		By whom?	By when?
Are the facilities for storing flammable substances adequate and safe?			
Are special precautions taken where naked flames are used?			
Is the use of LPG (bottled gas) heaters and appliances kept to a minimum, and where their use cannot be avoided, are users made aware of the dangers?			
Are wall-mounted heaters used rather than free-standing portable heaters?			
Are low flammability, fire-retardant materials used where there is an alternative, eg carpets, curtains, furniture and other furnishings?			
Have precautions been put in place to reduce the risk of arson?			
Do you check that the precautions you have established are actually being used and are effective?			

Fundraising

121 Fundraising is an important part of most charity and voluntary organisations. For some it is their main or only source of income and therefore vital to their survival.

122 Fundraising covers many different activities, from local park runs and fêtes through to bungee jumping, walking on hot coals or foreign mountain treks. While the charity or voluntary organisation will have control over its own fundraising events, many people 'do their own thing' without the charity being aware of what is happening or having any input or control.

Getting started

123 Health and safety must be included in all the pre-planning stages of every fundraising event. Regardless of the nature of the event, you need to think about:

- the venue – location, access points, size and inherent hazards, eg muddy ground, water features, abroad;
- the type of fundraising event or activity and the associated hazards;
- means of communication between key event personnel and the people attending – especially in emergencies;
- crowd numbers and control;
- stewards and marshals needed and their training;
- emergency plans, eg fire, first aid, evacuation of area and accident reporting;
- traffic control, particularly if people and vehicles are in the same area;
- disabled access and services;
- intended attractions, eg bouncy castles, gas balloons, animals;
- equipment needed, eg tables, gas cylinders;
- services needed, eg electricity, water, sound, lighting;
- food safety and hygiene (if food and drink are available).

124 All of these points must form part of your event risk assessments.

Further information

Working together on firework displays: A guide to safety for firework display organisers and operators HSG123 (Second edition) HSE Books 1999 ISBN 0 7176 2478 1

Giving your own firework display: How to run and fire it safely HSG124 (Second edition) HSE Books 2005 ISBN 0 7176 6162 8

Managing crowds safely: A guide for organisers at events and venues HSG154 (Second edition) HSE Books 2000 ISBN 0 7176 1834 X

The event safety guide: A guide to health, safety and welfare at music and similar events HSG195 (Second edition) HSE Books 1999 ISBN 0 7176 2453 6

HSE publishes a range of free Entertainment Information Sheets (ETIS), available from the HSE website.

Case study 17: Fête and dog show

A small local charity hosts an annual fête and fun dog show on the village cricket green. The fête attractions include a bouncy castle, various stalls, helium balloons and a barbeque food and drinks bar.

Hazards

- Crowds of people.
- Vehicles.
- Dogs – bites, allergies, phobias and faeces.
- Dangers associated with the attractions.
- Dangers associated with the grounds:
  - slips (mud or wet steps or paths);
  - water features;
  - steps and changes in ground level;
  - disabled access.
- Adverse weather conditions (hot and/or wet).
- Tents and marquees – stability and fire retardancy.
- Equipment, eg water boilers, trestle table stability.
- Moving and handling, eg during fête set up/take down.
- Trailing wires, eg from electrical wires for power to stalls and attractions.

Harm

- Injuries or ill health due to:
  - collisions between people and vehicles;
  - lack of crowd control, especially in emergencies;
  - dog bites, allergies etc;
  - falls from (and contact with other children on) the bouncy castle;
  - gas cylinders (balloons and barbeque food bar), eg pressurised gas, flammable gas;
  - tent or marquee collapse;
  - work equipment;
  - moving and handling loads;
  - trips;
  - hot weather (heat stroke);
  - the grounds.
- Fire.
- Food poisoning.

Solutions

- Include health and safety in all pre-event planning meetings, consider:
  - the suitability and size of the grounds and any obvious hazards – visit the location and liaise with the cricket club (they should ask for a copy of your risk assessment and vice versa);
  - the ground entrances and exits – take account of any disabled people who may attend;
  - the ground layout, especially where the stalls and attractions will be placed to minimise hazards – leave sufficient space around stalls etc for people to walk past safely;
  - a separate area for the dog show – how the dog areas will be cleaned up during and after the fête;
  - how people and vehicles will be separated – provide high-visibility clothing for workers in vehicle areas;
  - contacting the local police if any traffic control is needed on the nearby roads;
  - an effective means of communication during the fête – identify key personnel and emergency/
evacuation plans;
  - the estimated crowd numbers;
  - the necessary welfare facilities (eg toilets – include disabled facilities);
  - the necessary insurances.
- Check emergency arrangements:
  - fire – how and where will people be evacuated to in the event of a fire? What types of extinguishers are required in the different fête locations? Check workers are trained to use them. Separate fire extinguishers should be allocated for fundraising so they are not 'borrowed' from other work areas;
  - first aid – check if the venue has trained first aiders and suitable equipment available and that you are able to use them – if not, provide a first aider (eg an external provider such as St John Ambulance or the Red Cross);
  - accident reporting.
- Check all the identified hazards associated with the proposed attractions – ask the attraction suppliers for copies of their risk assessments.
- Where specialist attractions and equipment are required, establish whether the supplier will provide their own workers to manage the attractions or will they provide training for your workers.
- Ensure any workers or external food providers have current and valid food hygiene training certificates – take account of:
  - keeping raw and high-risk foods separate;
  - effective temperature control (insulating bags and ice packs are not sufficient for keeping food cold in hot weather);
  - how high-risk foods (eg meat products, ice cream) will be kept refrigerated and frozen;
  - how food handlers will wash their hands;
  - the washing of food equipment such as knives, ice cream scoops etc.

Notes

1   Consider how vulnerable people (eg children and disabled visitors) will be protected, as well as any workers, in the risk assessment.

2   The First Aid Regulations only require employers to provide first aid for employees at work – members of the public are not included. However, HSE recommends that suitable first-aid provision should be made where there is a reasonable likelihood that this will be needed – St John Ambulance and the British Red Cross can be booked to attend fundraising events. The revision of the Regulations continues to uphold this recommendation.

3   Trained first aiders providing first-aid treatment specifically to employees at work are covered by the Employers' Liability (Compulsory Insurance) Act 1969 – liability for treating other people should be checked and confirmed with your insurance company.

4   Fundraising extinguishers should be included in the annual workplace fire extinguisher service.

5   Always plan a 'debriefing' meeting soon after the event to discuss what went well or badly and why – this will lead to improvements in the future.

Case study 18: Talk to local Women's Institute (WI) group

The community fundraiser has been asked to present a short illustrated talk on the work of the charity to the local WI group in the church hall one evening. The only equipment available at the venue is an electric extension lead.

Hazards
- Unfamiliar venue.
- Moving and handling of equipment.
- Unknown safety standards of electric wiring and extension lead.
- Trailing wires.
- Work in darkness during presentation.
- Fire.
- Handling and carrying money donations.
- Out-of-hours working.

Harm
- Slips, trips and falls.
- Unable to escape in an emergency.
- Back injuries.
- Electric shock or electrocution.
- Assault.

Solutions
- Arrange to visit the premises before the event to see the parking available, the entrances and exits, general layout, escape routes and any relevant certificates, eg electrical wiring, insurance.
- Make a plan of where the equipment will be set up and where the audience will sit to minimise trailing wires and trips etc.
- Explain the fire and emergency arrangements at the beginning of the talk.
- Provide a trolley or bag on wheels to transport any equipment or get assistance – park as close as possible to where the equipment will be used.
- Check all the electrical equipment to look for loose wires, damaged cables, plugs.
- Provide an extension lead – this should be PAT tested.
- Provide a residual circuit breaker (RCB) – this is a device that plugs into the mains and that the extension lead then plugs into – it is designed to detect leaks in the electric supply and will turn off the power to the electric equipment.
- Request money donations to be given as cheques rather than cash.
- Carry any cash in inconspicuous bags – don't make it obvious and arrange for the worker to be escorted to the car.
- Send two workers to avoid lone working – if lone working is necessary, ensure there is a 'lone worker contact arrangement' in place, ie ensure there is someone else who knows where the worker is and when they are expected back.
- Provide personal safety training and (if required) personal alarms.
- Try and arrange talks during the day rather than in the evenings.

Case study 19: Pregnant women volunteering as event stewards

It is not uncommon to have pregnant women volunteering to help at various outdoor events (festivals etc).

Hazards
- Inappropriate work duties.

Harm
- Injuries to the women and/or their unborn babies.
- Miscarriage.
- Fatigue.

Solutions
- Avoid high-risk activities such as heavy lifting, anything that poses a threat of physical abuse or confrontation, prolonged standing etc.
- Plan their work to allow for rest breaks and if possible provide somewhere for them to take them.
- Control and limit the time they are actually at work.

Notes
1   HSE has produced detailed guidance on the hazards to new and expectant mothers and possible control measures.
2   Your duty extends to the safety of the unborn babies as well as to the women themselves.
3   You are legally required to carry out a risk assessment for all new and expectant mothers at work.

Case study 20: Fire-walking

A charity arranges for an external specialist company to manage a fire-walking (walking over hot coals) fundraising event on their behalf.

Hazards
- Hot coals – temperatures around 600 °C (1200 °F).
- Fire.
- Inappropriate information and preparation for the participants before the event.
- Incompetent external company.
- Poor event control.

Harm
- Serious burn injuries.
- Damage to property.

Solutions
- Use a reputable and competent fire-walking company – ask for and follow up references from organisations who have used them before.
- Have appropriate first aiders and equipment available – find out and agree who is responsible for providing this.
- Find out any prerequisites for the event, eg will the external company be present to manage and supervise the event throughout? Will any of the charity workers have responsibilities (do they need special training)? How much room is needed? How will the coals be heated and cooled down (is supervision after the event necessary)? How close can spectators stand?
- Ask for a copy of the external company's event risk assessment – this should form part of the charity's risk assessment.
- What emergency arrangements are needed and who is responsible for activating them?
- Check what insurances are required and that these are in date and valid – this applies to the charity and the external company.
- Ensure all participants are fully aware of:
  – the hazards;
  – the control measures;
  – any preparation routines – including things to avoid.

Notes
1   Specialist insurance cover may be required.
2   A fire-walker suffered serious burns to their feet because they had been for a pedicure (including treatment with oils) before the event – the oils were flammable and had soaked into the participant's feet.

Case study 21: Foreign mountain trek

An adventure holiday company offers foreign mountain treks to charities as sponsored fundraising opportunities.

Hazards
- Strenuous physical activities.
- High altitudes.
- Adverse weather.
- Infections.

Harm
- Fatigue.
- Falls from height.
- Altitude sickness.
- Cold and hypothermia.
- Foreign diseases.

Solutions
- Ensure the company is reputable, competent and experienced in the type of mountain trekking and the country being visited – ask for and follow up references from organisations who have used them before.
- Ensure that the charity participants are accompanied at all times by competent guides who are familiar with local conditions.
- Ask for a copy of the external company's event risk assessment – this should form part of the charity's risk assessment.
- What emergency arrangements are in place for dealing with any injuries or illnesses, including travel arrangements for getting participants home to the UK?
- Effective means of communication with participants and with the UK charity bases.
- Check what insurances are required and that these are in-date and valid – this applies to the charity and the external company.
- Ensure all participants are fully aware of:
  – the hazards associated with the activity;
  – the necessary control measures;
  – any pre-event preparation routines:
    - any previous experience needed;
    - level of fitness required and how to build up to it – consider how long this will take;
    - specialist equipment required;
    - any vaccinations required – again, consider the length of time needed;
    - necessary visas etc;
    - things to avoid.

Notes
1   Specialist insurance cover may be necessary.
2   The organising company should provide detailed information packs on the points above.

Figure 6 Fundraising events flow chart

Have all health and safety issues associated with your event been identified in your pre-event planning meetings?

Yes | **No**

Do (or could) any of the following factors apply to your fundraising event? (The lists are not exhaustive.)

People

- Designated stewards.
- Numbers expected.
- Entry controls.
- Communication.
- Vehicle control – designated pedestrian routes.
- Emergency procedures.

Event

- Nature of event.
- Required space.
- Equipment hire/erection/use.
- Special training.
- Specialist events and/or equipment (eg gas cylinders).
- Control of animals/children.
- Protective devices.
- Handling cash.

Facilities

- Adequate toilets.
- First-aid provision.
- Emergency assembly point.
- Electrical supply (electrical safety, trailing wires).
- Disabled access.
- Central information point.
- Lighting/PA systems.
- Refuse collection.
- Insurances.

Environment

- Size and layout.
- Suitability for event.
- Uneven ground.
- Weather effects – hot/cold/wet.
- Steps and slopes.
- Site access/exit.
- Flow systems for visitors/vehicles.
- Vehicle parking.
- Emergency access.

Have these health and safety issues been risk assessed?

Yes

Have all the associated risks been removed or controlled?

Yes

Take action to do so. ← **Yes** ← Can you do anything about these factors to remove or reduce the risk of injury?

No

Keep under review and revise if necessary.

The risk is **unacceptable** – consider getting help.

Table 7 Management checklist: Fundraising (continued)

Checkpoints	Yes, No or N/A	Action required	
		By whom?	By when?
Is there a named person responsible for taking the lead on the event and who will co-ordinate the risk assessment? (See chapter *Managing health and safety and risk assessment*.)			
Before agreeing the site/activity			
Is health and safety part of the pre-event planning meetings?			
Has the site been assessed as suitable?			
Have necessary permissions been obtained?			
Have the local authority and/or police been contacted regarding impact on local traffic conditions?			
Is the site easily accessible to the public?			
What is the maximum number of people the site can safely accommodate?			
Are toilet facilities available – or can Portaloos be set up?			
General considerations			
Are first-aid facilities available?			
Are there procedures for reporting and recording any accidents or near misses? (See chapter *Accidents, sickness absence and returning to work*.)			
If refreshments will be available, are providers qualified to meet food hygiene regulations? Are hand-washing facilities available? Are portable fire extinguishers needed?			
Are there contingency plans for bad weather?			
Is additional insurance cover required?			
Are arrangements in place to handle and bank money? Are extra security measures needed?			
Are there a sufficient number of competent/professional stewards available, who are briefed as to what is expected of them, including emergency procedures?			
Specialist activities (eg bouncy castles, helicopter rides, abseiling, firework displays, fire-walking, bungee jumping)			
Are the people leading on the activity properly qualified?			
Are they experienced in this sort of activity?			
Do they have a comprehensive risk assessment?			
Are there adequate emergency procedures?			
Have they considered weather implications?			
Do they have insurance cover?			

Table 7 Management checklist: Fundraising (continued)

Checkpoints	Yes, No or N/A	Action required	
		By whom?	By when?
Equipment			
Is all equipment in a safe condition for use, especially use of electrical equipment outdoors? (See chapter *Work equipment*.)			
Site layout			
Ensure pedestrians and vehicles are segregated.			
Avoid trip and slip hazards.			
Ensure specialist activities are segregated from the public.			
Clearing up			
Has the site been left in the same condition as when it was taken over, with all waste correctly disposed of?			
Review			
Is there a process to review the success of the activity and to take note of any learning points for future occasions?			

Warning
Contains
asbestos

Breathing asbestos
dust is dangerous
to health

Hazardous substances

125 Nearly all workplaces will use or produce some kind of hazardous substance. This chapter explains what hazardous substances are and gives you several different scenarios to help you identify if you have any hazardous substances.

What are hazardous substances?

126 Hazardous substances are any substances capable of causing illness (eg hepatitis or cancer) or some other adverse health effect (eg dermatitis). They may be chemicals which have been classed as 'toxic, very toxic, corrosive, irritant or harmful' but may also be infections (such as bacteria and viruses) or large quantities of dust. It is also important to consider allergies, eg workers may be allergic to the latex in some rubber gloves.

127 The laws covering hazardous substances at work are known as the Control of Substances Hazardous to Health Regulations 2002 – you may know them as the 'COSHH' Regulations.

128 Asbestos is not included in COSHH because it has its own set of laws, although the general information in this chapter is relevant. Substances that cause fires or explosions are also excluded from COSHH, although you must still carry out relevant risk assessments if they are present in your work activities.

Why are hazardous substances important?

129 Hazardous substances can cause serious illnesses, some of which may be fatal or incurable, eg HIV. They may also cause permanent or temporary disabilities. At the very least, they can cause discomfort and soreness.

130 They often take a very long time to show any symptoms; in the case of some cancers, it can take 40 years or more for the illness to show up.

What do you have to do

131 You will have to identify all of your work activities that either use and/or produce hazardous substances. For each hazardous substance you identify, you must carry out a risk assessment. This assessment will:

- identify who is likely to come into contact with that substance (it might not just be your workers, eg residents or patients may also be at risk) and if they are especially vulnerable, eg pregnant women;

- identify how it will get into the body, eg by breathing it, swallowing it or through the skin;
- indicate what the possible result of that contact will be;
- identify if the risk is unacceptable and that you will need to do more to protect people.

132 If you use dangerous chemicals, your supplier should give you the 'safety data sheets' for the chemicals that you have bought. These sheets contain all the safety, use and storage and first-aid information about that chemical – you should keep them in a file where people can look at them.

133 Once you have removed or reduced the risks, you must regularly review your risk assessments and revise them.

134 You must also keep any worker health records for 40 years. It may also be useful to keep any associated information (such as risk assessments) for 40 years as well – this information may be relevant in future court cases to prove hazards were identified and controlled.

Further information

Control of substances hazardous to health (Fifth edition). The Control of Substances Hazardous to Health Regulations 2002 (as amended). Approved Code of Practice and guidance L5 (Fifth edition) HSE Books 2005 ISBN 0 7176 2981 3

COSHH a brief guide to the Regulations: What you need to know about the Control of Substances Hazardous to Health Regulations 2002 (COSHH) Leaflet INDG136(rev3) HSE Books 2005 (single copy free or priced packs of 10 ISBN 0 7176 2982 1)

COSHH essentials: Easy steps to control chemicals (Third edition) HSE Books 2006 Web version: www.hse.gov.uk

Preventing dermatitis at work: Advice for employers and employees Leaflet INDG233 HSE Books 1996 (single copy free or priced packs of 15 ISBN 0 7176 1246 5)

New and expectant mothers at work: A guide for employers HSG122 (Second edition) HSE Books 2002 ISBN 0 7176 2583 4

Infections in the workplace to new and expectant mothers HSE Books 1997 ISBN 0 7176 1360 7

Case study 22: Cleaning products

A new cleaner, working in a residential home for people with learning difficulties, decanted some caustic chemical from its original container into an empty lemonade bottle. This bottle was left unattended on a corridor table while she cleaned inside a resident's bedroom.

Hazards
- Contact with and/or exposure to hazardous chemical.

Harm
- Residents drink contents and suffer internal chemical burns.
- Any person passing by accidentally knocks the bottle over and the chemical splashes onto them causing skin and/or eye burns.

Solutions
- Use safer alternative chemicals.
- Restrict use of dangerous chemicals to staff who have been specifically authorised to use them.
- Ensure chemicals are never left unattended:
  - provide smaller trays for carrying essential cleaning items that can be taken into the rooms;
  - provide a trolley with a lockable area where the chemicals can be securely kept when not in use.
- Ensure chemical containers always have a tamper-proof lid on when they are not being used.
- Ensure all new staff are supervised until you are sure that they are competent to do the work.
- Ensure staff are trained in the following, and keep training records:
  - familiarisation of the workplace, policies and procedures (induction training);
  - COSHH (handling, use and storage of chemicals);
  - the control measures identified by the COSHH risk assessment.

Notes
1   A nursing home was fined £40 000 plus £6000 costs for leaving a caustic chemical in a water jug where a resident was able to drink it – the resident subsequently died.
2   In a similar situation, a youth centre was permanently closed after a three-year-old child drank some kettle descaler (which looked like a fizzy orange drink) left in the kitchen. The child died.

Case study 23: Laundry

A hospice in-house laundry has to wash bed linen soiled with blood and other body fluids.

Hazards
- Contact with blood and body fluids.

Harm
- Infections.
- Contamination.

Solutions
- Clear procedures for handling soiled linen and items – follow the universal precautions for infection control:
  - physical barriers, eg gloves, plasters over open wounds etc;
  - regular and thorough hand washing;
  - regular and effective cleaning;
  - training and awareness.
- Use of red soluble[Note 1] sacks to minimise handling.
- Provision and use of personal protective clothing, eg gloves and aprons.
- Suitable and maintained washing machines.

Notes
1   These are special sacks that dissolve in the washing machine during the wash cycle. Soiled linen is put straight into these sacks from the beds and then put directly into the washing machine – they stop the need for multiple handling and subsequent sluice washes to remove the soiling before machine washing.

Case study 24: Dusts

A worker at a horse and donkey sanctuary regularly assists with exercising the horses in the indoor riding school and other associated duties, including filling up all the hay sacks from the loose hay in the barn.

Hazards
- Large quantities of dust from the indoor school floor covering and the hay.
- Mould spores in the hay.

Harm
- Breathing problems, including asthma.
- Allergies.
- Anaphylactic shock (very severe allergic reaction) to the mould spores.

Solutions
- Damp down the indoor school floor and hay before use to reduce the amount of dust in the air.
- Make sure these tasks are assigned to workers who are not susceptible to breathing problems and do not suffer from allergies.
- Provide suitable face masks for these activities.

Notes
1   Exposures to significant amounts of dust are covered by the COSHH Regulations.
2   You will also need to address any other adverse effects such as asthma or allergies.
3   Other work activities where large quantities of dust are formed include saw mills, paper mills or stores etc.

Case study 25: Engine oils

A volunteer mechanic working for a motorbike museum has to regularly take apart, clean and reassemble old motorbike engines. His hands are exposed to the oil and dirt associated with used engines and he has to use a special decreasing agent to clean his hands during the day.

Hazards
- Skin contact with hazardous substances.

Harm
- Dermatitis.
- Cancer.

Solutions
- Clean engine parts as much as possible before dismantling and/or use cleaning tanks with lifting equipment etc to minimise contact with chemicals.
- Check for and (if possible) provide safer engine and hand cleaning agents.
- Provide protective gloves for work on engines.
- Keep open wounds covered with waterproof plasters.
- Regular self-examination of hands for signs of dryness, cracks etc.
- Occupational health or health surveillance programmes for workers exposed to these chemicals.

Case study 26: Natural infections

Conservation volunteers are asked to carry out some ground maintenance work in and around a woodland pond.

Hazards
- Contact with potentially contaminated water.
- Contact with soil.
- Possible contact with deer ticks and other insects.

Harm
- Potential for open skin wounds and injuries.
- Weil's disease.
- Infections and other contamination from soil.
- Lyme disease.

Solutions
- Tetanus vaccines for high-risk workers.
- Cover all open wounds with waterproof plasters – provide a first-aid kit for remote workers.
- Provide suitable personal protective clothing.
- Training to cover identified hazards, symptoms of possible diseases and main principles of infection control.
- Access to health surveillance programmes.

Notes
1   Weil's disease is caused by stagnant or slow-running water that has become contaminated with rat urine.
2   Lyme disease is caused when people working or walking in the countryside are bitten by deer ticks, which pass the infective agent directly into the bloodstream.
3   Soil contains a wide number of potentially harmful bacteria and parasites, eg parasitic worms. One of the most commonly known infections in soil is tetanus.

Case study 27: Legionella (water systems)

During a routine inspection of a residential care home for the elderly by a local EHO, it was noted that the shower in the upstairs bathroom was never used and was clogged with scale. When asked for the legionella risk assessment, the manager was unable to produce it and did not know when the water system was last tested and cleaned.

Hazards
- Build up of legionella bacteria in the water system.
- Dispersal of bacteria in water droplets and aerosols from the shower head.

Harm
- Outbreak of legionnaires' disease among vulnerable residents (could also affect workers and visitors).
- Severe illness or deaths from legionnaires' disease.
- Civil and criminal prosecution.
- Loss of reputation.

Solutions
- Design high-risk areas out of water systems, eg dead ends in pipework, unused water tanks.
- Annual legionella risk assessment by a specialist contractor.
- Planned preventative maintenance programme for building water systems – including appropriate water treatment such as chlorination and regular running and descaling of shower heads.
- Maintaining hot water systems[Note 4] above 50 °C and cold water systems below 20 °C to minimise legionella bacteria growth.
- Regular sampling and analysis of various water outlets for presence of legionella bacteria.

Notes
1   Legionnaires' disease is also commonly associated with the evaporative units and cooling towers of air conditioning plants. If you have any of these, they must be included in your legionella risk assessments and be part of a planned preventative maintenance programme.
2   Any water features, eg garden fountains etc, in the workplace should also be included in the legionella risk assessments.
3   Regular samples should be taken and analysed in a laboratory to confirm or otherwise the presence of legionella bacteria.
4   Hot water temperatures will need to be thermostatically controlled to 43 °C at all outlets used by patients or clients to prevent accidental scalding.

Figure 7 Hazardous substances flow chart

Have you identified all the hazardous substances used in or produced by your work activities?

Yes   **No**

Are any of your workers likely to be exposed to or come into contact with any of the following?
(These lists are **not** exhaustive.)

Chemicals

- Toxic, very toxic.
- Corrosive.
- Irritant.
- Harmful.

Harm:

- dermatitis;
- allergies;
- chemical burns;
- respiratory problems;
- cancers.

Precautions:

- use safer alternatives;
- ventilation: local exhaust/general;
- good room ventilation;
- provide PPE, eg gloves, glasses.

Infections

Sources:

- blood and body fluids, eg HIV, hepatitis;
- water/air conditioning systems, eg legionella bacteria;
- ponds/lakes, eg Weil's disease;
- soil, eg tetanus;
- tick bites, eg Lyme disease.

Universal precautions:

- physical barriers, eg gloves, wound plasters;
- hand washing;
- cleanliness/cleaning;
- awareness and training;
- vaccinations.

Dusts

Sources:

- saw mills;
- paper storage areas;
- laundries;
- hay/straw, mould spores, dry dust;
- angle-grinding;
- demolition works.

Harm:

- respiratory problems;
- sore eyes.

Precautions:

- appropriate ventilation;
- equipment maintenance;
- cleanliness/housekeeping;
- provide PPE, eg masks.

For each substance, identify:

- Who will be affected by that substance?
- Is the exposure ongoing or a 'one off'?
- How will that substance get into the body (breathing, drinking, through the skin, through an open wound)?
- What are the possible dangers?
- How likely are those dangers to occur?

Have you carried out a risk assessment for each of the hazardous substances identified?   **No** → Take action or get advice – the health risks may be **unacceptable.**

Yes

Have you taken sufficient precautions to remove or control the associated risks?   **Yes** → Have you recorded your risk assessment findings?

Yes

You will need to keep health records for 40 years – it is good practice to keep other related information as well. ← Keep your risk assessments under review and revise your precautions when necessary.

Table 8 Management checklist: Hazardous substances

Checkpoints	Yes, No or N/A	Action required	
		By whom?	By when?
Chemicals			
Do you use any chemicals at work?			
Do any of your work activities create hazardous substances, eg fumes, dusts?			
Could any of your workers come into contact with these chemicals?			
Could someone other than your workers come into contact with chemicals, eg residents, children, visitors, contractors?			
If you have contractors working on site, do you know what chemicals they are using or storing and have you requested copies of their risk assessments for any effects on your workers?			
Are any of your workers exposed to large amounts of dust?			
Do you (or could you) have any pregnant workers coming into contact with chemicals?			
Do any of your workers have breathing problems or weaknesses, eg asthma?			
Do any of your workers suffer from allergies?			
If you answered 'yes' to any of the above, have you carried out a risk assessment on **each** hazardous substance?			
Have you taken precautions to remove or minimise the risks, and are your workers aware of these?			
Do you regularly review these assessments?			
Do you have procedures in place to report and clean up spillages immediately?			
Do you have a file of safety data sheets for all your hazardous chemicals?			
Is this file of safety data sheets regularly checked against the chemicals you have on the premises?			
Are your workers trained to understand any dangers associated with the chemicals they may come into contact with, and the necessary precautions?			
Do your workers understand the safety information on chemical container labels, and know where/how to get further information?			
Infections			
Are your workers likely to come into contact with blood or other body fluids, eg vomit, urine or faeces?			
Are your workers likely to come into contact with external water features, eg ponds, ditches, lakes etc?			
Do any of your workers work in gardens, parks or other outdoor environments?			
Do any of your workers work with animals or in animal environments?			

Table 8 Management checklist: Hazardous substances (continued)

Checkpoints	Yes, No or N/A	Action required	
		By whom?	By when?
Could your work activities involve exposure to other infectious agents, eg bacteria, viruses, parasites?			
Could some one other than your workers come into contact with work-related infections?			
Do you (or could you) have any pregnant workers coming into contact with infections?			
Do any of your workers suffer from latex allergies (latex may be found in disposable protective gloves, plasters etc)?			
If you answered 'yes' to any of the above, have you carried out a risk assessment for **each** such exposure?			
Have you taken precautions to remove or minimise the risks, and are your workers aware of these?			
Do you regularly review these assessments?			
Do you have procedures in place to report and clean up body fluid etc spillages immediately?			
Are the hot and cold water systems in your building regularly checked, sampled and treated?			
Do you take regular hot water temperature checks from various outlets in the building?			
Are your workers trained to understand any dangers associated with work-related infections they may come into contact with and the necessary precautions?			
Do your workers know and understand the 'universal precautions'? (See Figure 7.)			
Do you have procedures for the safe handling and treatment of soiled linen, clothing, dressings or furnishings?			
Do you have an effective procedure for disposing of clinical waste?			
Health monitoring			
Do you have a system where workers can report any adverse health effects (in confidence if necessary)?			
Do you have access to occupational health services or health surveillance schemes if your workers suffer any ill effects from hazardous substances?			
Have you kept all relevant records relating to exposure to or contact with hazardous substances? This includes any worker health records, maintenance records, risk assessments, and policies and procedures.			
Health records must be kept for 40 years (it is good practice to keep all the other associated information for 40 years as well) – do you have arrangements in place to meet this requirement?			

Lone working

135 Many charities will have workers who work on their own at some time. This is common in charities providing carers for people at home, or charities involved with conservation and wildlife work. However, it may also apply to workers in charity shops if their colleagues haven't turned up for work or to workers who stay late to finish off some work after everyone else has left the office building.

136 Regardless of the different situations and hazards, there are common factors that will always apply, including:

- having a lone worker policy;
- avoiding lone working where possible;
- knowing that lone working is occurring and carrying out risk assessments;
- having contact arrangements in place so that someone knows the whereabouts and schedule of the lone worker and can start emergency procedures if necessary;
- providing adequate first-aid equipment;
- avoiding particularly hazardous activities, eg using dangerous equipment or unfamiliar tasks.

Lone working in private homes

137 Lone working often occurs away from the employer's workplace in private homes. In these situations, the employer has no control over the workplace and cannot require hazards to be controlled. This means there is a responsibility on the lone worker to identify these hazards and take the appropriate precautions. Ultimately, it may mean withdrawing services until improvements are made – if a worker takes this decision it is important for management to support them. Likewise, it is important for management to prevent workers continuing to work in dangerous environments when these have been identified.

138 Again, there are some simple points to consider:

- Pre-plan and get as much information as possible before making the first visit – share information with other organisations visiting that home.
- Where the home to be visited is located:
  - Is it in a high-risk area?
  - Is the area well lit?
    Can workers park close by (avoid public car parks and isolated spots)?
  - Is public transport nearby if the worker cannot drive?
- Time of the visit – try to keep to hours when people are likely to be around, eg avoid night visits.

- Where are the exits from the home in an emergency – is the address written down in case the emergency services have to be called?
- Who is likely to be present during the visit?
- Are any animals likely to be present?
- Does the person being visited, or any other people likely to be present, have a history of aggression or violence?
- What equipment needs to be carried? Consider moving and handling issues.
- Have a schedule of visits and expected durations – a copy should be kept with the named contact person.
- Provide 'global positioning satellite' (GPS) mobile phones for workers in remote outdoor locations – in an emergency, their location could be accurately tracked.

Personal safety

139 Workers who work on their own should be made aware of these general tips on personal safety:

- know what the contact arrangements are and who to contact in an emergency;
- be aware of who is, and what is happening, around you at all times;
- keep valuables out of sight in your vehicle – put them in the car boot before you leave, not when you get there;
- always leave plenty of room between you and the car in front when waiting in traffic, so you can get away easily;
- reverse into parking spots so you can get away easily;
- walk confidently – hands out of pockets;
- keep to well-lit public areas;
- if intimidated while driving, continue to the nearest police station or public area, eg petrol station;
- keep the car doors locked while driving;
- know where you are going and the route to take – have an alternative route in case of delays.

Further information

Working alone in safety: Controlling the risks of solitary work Leaflet INDG73(rev) HSE Books 1998 (single copy free or priced packs of 15 ISBN 0 7176 1507 3)

A series of real life case studies offering practical ways to reduce the threat of violence to lone workers are available on HSE's website at www.hse.gov.uk/violence.

The Suzy Lamplugh Trust has also produced a wide range of useful publications and guidance on personal safety – see Appendix 1: *Useful contacts*.

Case study 28: Work in a private home and contact arrangements

A domiciliary care worker needs to visit people's homes at night to provide support. The area is poorly lit and the worker raises concerns about their personal safety.

Hazards
- Lone working.
- Getting lost in and/or unfamiliar with the area.
- Slips or falls in poorly lit area.
- Possible assault.
- Inability to seek assistance.

Harm
- Verbal assault.
- Aggression.
- Violence.
- Hostage taking.
- Abduction.
- Theft.
- Unable to provide the support to the person when needed.
- Anxiety and stress for the care worker.
- Increased likelihood of an accident or injury occurring.
- Increased liability.

Solutions
- Carry out a risk assessment with the worker to assess the actual and potential risks and inform them of the necessary control measures.
- Provide clear directions to the location.
- Provide a means of lighting, eg torch.
- Provide personal panic alarms.
- Provide means to summon assistance, eg mobile phone.
- Provide training in personal safety and lone working to all the staff affected.
- Introduce a contact arrangements system (buddy system) so the worker's whereabouts are known and action can be taken if necessary.

Notes
1   Some local authorities and private organisations provide a lone worker monitoring service. Lone workers register onto the service and complete a registration form that contains relevant information such as date of birth, general description of the worker, car details etc – anything that would help to identify the worker.

The lone worker phones into the monitoring centre before they start their visits and gives a list of the addresses or locations that they will be visiting, along with estimated visit durations. They confirm a time to report back into the monitoring centre when they have finished. If the lone worker reports back on or before the confirmed time, the details are removed from the monitoring system. If they fail to make the agreed call, the monitoring centre allows a defined and agreed delay period before calling the worker's contact telephone number(s) given on the registration form. If the worker confirms they are safe and well, the information is again taken out of the system. If the worker doesn't answer, then the next specified person is notified and/or the police.

Where the risk is unknown, ie a first visit, or where it is assessed as being high risk, access to a mobile phone with satellite tracking (GPS phones) may be considered. Some GPS phones allow an emergency link with the monitoring centre by pressing one button – the monitoring centre may either be instructed to answer, or not to speak unless the worker requests them to. Once this is activated, the monitoring centre can hear what is going on through the phone and the satellite tracking system will confirm the phone's location.

Case study 29: Personal safety

A volunteer worker visited a known client in his own home as a 'befriender'. She had noticed during her last visit that the client seemed agitated and 'not his usual self'. During this visit she became seriously concerned about his behaviour; his speech was slurred, he was unkempt and she thought she could smell alcohol on his breath. While making a cup of tea, she noticed an empty whisky bottle in the waste bin. The client, furious that she had seen the whisky bottle, shook her by the shoulders and locked the back door to prevent her leaving. Eventually, after several hours, she did manage to unbolt the back door and make her escape, but he followed her into the garden. Fortunately, she was able to shout for help and a next-door neighbour phoned for the police. After almost an hour's negotiation the client allowed the police in to the house.

Hazards
- Lone working – no assistance or back up.
- Irrational and unpredictable client – alcohol abuse.
- Assumption of safety as client was known to worker.
- No contact arrangements.
- No follow up or refresher training.
- Poor incident reporting.

Harm
- Injuries.
- Stress and trauma.
- Sickness absence.
- Workload to be covered by other workers.
- Loss of experienced worker – on return to work, moved to another role.

Solutions
- Update of case files to record and monitor changes in behaviour.
- Share of information, including effective incident reporting procedures.
- Induction and subsequent training throughout period of work – frequent refresher training.
- Contact procedures – if these had been in place, action would have been taken much sooner to rescue the worker.
- Withdrawal of service in high-risk cases.
- Worker support, eg counselling.

Case study 30: Late office worker

A charity office worker stays late into the evening to catch up on their backlog of work.

- Hazards
- Lone working.
- Office hazards:
  - work equipment;
  - electricity;
  - slips and trips;
  - display screen equipment use.
- Poor security measures:
  - building security;
  - personal safety.
- Fire.
- Lack of first-aid provision.

Harm
- Injuries associated with the hazard list – untreated if there is no first-aid available.
- Aggression and violence from intruders.
- Theft.
- Building and property damage due to fire.

Solutions
- Ensure effective communication with the worker to monitor workloads and if/when they become a problem, establish the reasons why the overload occurred, eg unrealistic volume of work or worker capabilities etc. **Take action to avoid the situation getting worse or arising in the future**.
- Reorganise and reprioritise the workload.
- Try to arrange for the worker to complete any essential work at home, ie provide a laptop computer – re-enforce display screen equipment precautions, especially working/sitting posture and work breaks.
- Ensure effective contact arrangements are in place if workers stay late in the office, even if it is a rare occurrence – providing a mobile phone and a contact number may be sufficient.
- Ensure the worker knows what to do in the event of a fire or needing first-aid treatment.
- Re-emphasise hazards and control measures associated with office work.
- Ensure the building is secure and cannot be entered from outside without the worker's knowledge or permission.

Notes
1   Late working is a common occurrence in many office environments but very few have specific arrangements to protect those workers who do stay late and may be on their own.

Case study 31: Remote worker

Wildlife charity workers carry out evening/night patrols to monitor and protect wildlife activity in the surrounding countryside. Because of the sensitivity of the wildlife they monitor, they split up after the briefing meeting and individually patrol their designated areas.

Hazards
- Lone working.
- Darkness.
- Aggression or violence (eg from poachers).
- Adverse weather.
- Lack of welfare facilities, eg toilets.

Harm
- Trips, slips and falls.
- Assault-related injuries and trauma.
- Injuries from contact with tree branches etc.
- Ill health associated with exposure to adverse weather.
- Infections, eg Lyme disease from deer ticks.

Solutions
- Agree and inform the workers of the contact arrangements in the case of emergencies – this may be by whistle or mobile phone among the other workers, or arrangements with an external monitoring company.
- Arrange for workers to meet up at set times during their shift.
- Confirm workers have the necessary physical fitness levels.
- Provide torches.
- Provide individual pocket first-aid kits.
- Train workers in dealing with difficult people.
- Provide necessary personal protective clothing for the adverse weather, eg waterproofs, thermal clothing.

Figure 8 Lone working flow chart

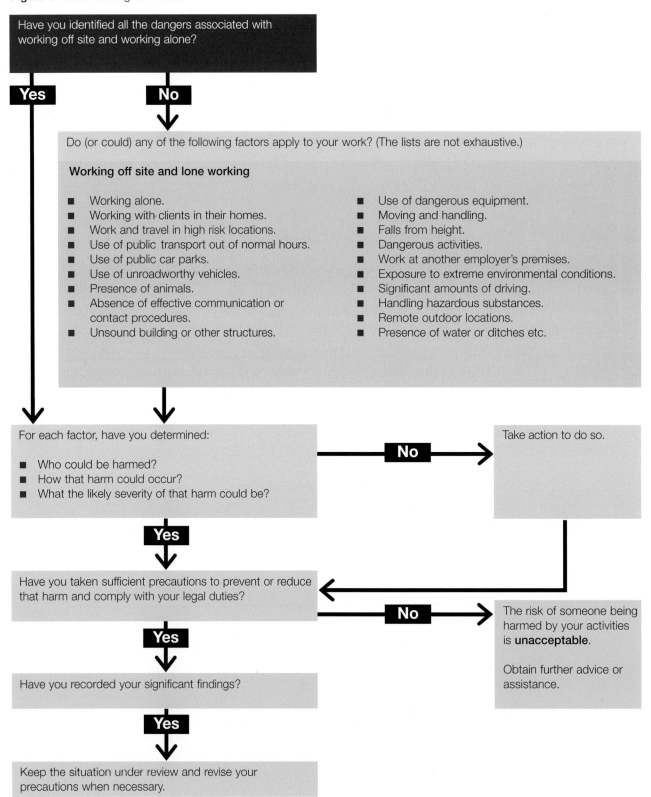

Have you identified all the dangers associated with working off site and working alone?

Yes **No**

Do (or could) any of the following factors apply to your work? (The lists are not exhaustive.)

Working off site and lone working

- Working alone.
- Working with clients in their homes.
- Work and travel in high risk locations.
- Use of public transport out of normal hours.
- Use of public car parks.
- Use of unroadworthy vehicles.
- Presence of animals.
- Absence of effective communication or contact procedures.
- Unsound building or other structures.

- Use of dangerous equipment.
- Moving and handling.
- Falls from height.
- Dangerous activities.
- Work at another employer's premises.
- Exposure to extreme environmental conditions.
- Significant amounts of driving.
- Handling hazardous substances.
- Remote outdoor locations.
- Presence of water or ditches etc.

For each factor, have you determined:

- Who could be harmed?
- How that harm could occur?
- What the likely severity of that harm could be?

No → Take action to do so.

Yes

Have you taken sufficient precautions to prevent or reduce that harm and comply with your legal duties?

No → The risk of someone being harmed by your activities is **unacceptable**.

Obtain further advice or assistance.

Yes

Have you recorded your significant findings?

Yes

Keep the situation under review and revise your precautions when necessary.

Table 9 Management checklist: Lone working

Checkpoints	Yes, No or N/A	Action required	
		By whom?	By when?

Does your risk assessment include:
 	
■ Is lone working the only option?
■ Can a lone worker do the work safely?
■ Is the worker fit for the task (medically, physically and through competence)?
■ Is sufficient information/training/instruction given to workers?
■ Are young/inexperienced workers particularly at risk?
■ Are pregnant workers at risk?
■ Are there agreed means of communication:
  — in an emergency;
  — when circumstances change; or
  — at the end of the working day?
■ What happens if the worker has an accident or is taken ill?
■ Are suitable first-aid facilities available (eg travel kit)?
■ Are toilets and facilities for drinks/meals available?
■ Is there a risk of aggression or violence:
  — from cash handling;
  — from clients/members of the public; or
  — from pets/animals?
■ Would changing weather conditions affect the worker's safety:
  — when carrying out the work activities; or
  — while travelling?			

Have you put the necessary precautions and procedures in place to control the risks identified?			
Have you recorded the assessment findings?			
Are these findings communicated to all workers affected?			
Are systems in place to monitor the safety of lone workers?			
Is there an agreed emergency procedure if a worker raises the alarm, or fails to report in or log off at the agreed time?			
Do you review your risk assessments after all accidents/incidents?			
Are appointments made in advance and during working normal hours?			
Do you check that the precautions you have established are actually being used and are effective?			

Moving and handling

140 Each year in Great Britain, over a million people suffer from musculoskeletal disorders (MSDs), such as backache or upper limb pain, caused or made worse by their work. In 2004/05, an estimated 11.6 million working days were lost in this way. Back injuries caused by moving and handling loads are one of the most common reasons for workers taking time off work.

141 You may also see moving and handling called manual handling. The term 'musculoskeletal disorders' (MSDs) is often used for injuries caused by moving and handling loads.

142 Moving and handling are about using your body to lift, move, hold or support a load manually. Loads may be alive (eg people or animals – 'animate' loads) or they may be objects (eg boxes, furniture – 'inanimate' loads).

143 Moving and handling includes:

- lifting;
- carrying;
- pulling;
- pushing;
- static holding (holding in one position);
- lowering;
- reaching/stretching;
- supporting.

144 The Manual Handling Operations Regulations 1992 (as amended) (MHOR) cover manual handling. The requirements of these Regulations can be summarised:

- remove risks of injury associated with moving and handling activities;
- if you can't remove the injury risks, then you assess them;
- take the necessary measures to reduce the risk of injury to the lowest level possible;
- inform, instruct and train your workers in moving and handling.

Assessing moving and handling activities

145 The first question that should always be asked is 'is this moving and handling activity necessary?' If the activity is not necessary, it can be avoided and is therefore not an injury risk. If the activity is necessary, it must be assessed to find the safest way of doing it.

146 There are four factors that you must consider when carrying out a moving and handling assessment:

- **L**oad – what is being carried or moved?
- **I**ndividual – who is moving and/or handling the load?
- **T**ask – what does the activity actually involve, how will it be undertaken?
- **E**nvironment – where will the moving and handling activity be carried out?

Note: the first letter of these four factors (L, I, T, E) make the word LITE – this may help you to remember what you need to think about.

147 Figure 9 gives some of the individual points you need to think about in your assessment for each of these four factors. There are a number of reasonably low-cost pieces of equipment available that can make load handling much easier. Sack barrows, trolleys, containers with handles etc can very often be used to help control the risk of injury. Using hire shops can be a useful way of trying out a particular device or a way of providing something that is not needed frequently. See HSE's free leaflet *Are you making the best use of lifting and handling aids* INDG398.

148 The risk assessment process is basically the same for inanimate loads, moving animals or moving people. However, if you are moving people, there are other important issues to consider, eg:

- Can they help themselves in any way?
- Can they understand and react to what you say to them?
- Do they have any medical conditions, eg catheters, that make handling more difficult?

149 This guidance booklet does not give sufficient information to cover all aspects of handling people, more specialist information can be obtained from HSE guidance *Handling home care* HSG225 and in the RCN/Backcare booklet *The guide to the handling of people*. Workers assisting with the mobility of people/moving or handling people must have special and regular training in the correct techniques.

150 Extra specialist moving and handling training may also be necessary in some inanimate cases, eg moving furniture. Charity shops that receive and deliver furniture should consider training their workers in the correct handling techniques. The British Association of Removers (BAR) can provide this sort of training – see Appendix 1: *Useful contacts*.

Further information

Manual handling.Manual Handling Operations Regulations 1992 (as amended). Guidance on Regulations L23 (Third edition) HSE Books 2004 ISBN 0 7176 2823 X

Manual handling: Solutions you can handle HSG115 HSE Books 1994 ISBN 0 7176 0693 7

A pain in your workplace? Ergonomic problems and solutions HSG121 HSE Books 1994 ISBN 0 7176 0668 6

Handling home care: Achieving safe, efficient and positive outcomes for care workers and clients HSG225 HSE Books 2002 ISBN 0 7176 2228 2

Getting to grips with manual handling: A short guide Leaflet INDG143(rev2) HSE Books 2004 (single copy free or priced packs of 15 ISBN 0 7176 2828 0)

Are you making the best use of lifting and handling aids? Leaflet INDG398 HSE Books 2004 (single copy free or priced packs of 15 ISBN 0 7176 2900 7)

Manual handling assessment tool – on the HSE website www.hse.gov.uk

The guide to the handling of people (Fifth edition) RCN/Backcare 2005

Case study 32: Sorting donated goods

The manager of a charity shop asked a volunteer to help out with the sorting of donated goods because the worker who normally did this was off sick with a back problem. The volunteer was advised to ask for help if anything was too heavy or awkward to move by herself, and left to her task. She asked for help to move a heavy box of goods and later wanted to replace the half empty box on the top shelf before she went home. Because she was in a hurry, she did not go into the back of the shop to get the stepladder but stood on the shelving to slide the box back onto the top shelf. She overreached and dropped the box. She managed to stop herself from falling down, but twisted her back in holding her balance. Feeling a bit silly about it, she did not tell anyone at the time. The next day she had been due to go on holiday to stay with her daughter, but because of her injury had to cancel. Staff at the shop were unaware of the accident until the volunteer's daughter phoned to say that her mother would not be returning to the shop to work because of her back injury, and that she was taking legal advice on behalf of her mother.

Hazards
- Moving and handling.
- Work at height.
- Incorrect and unsafe work practices.

Harm
- Back injury to worker.
- Loss of good volunteer and goodwill.
- Bad publicity – local newspaper.
- Lengthy enforcement investigation – possible enforcement action, eg improvement notice.
- Cost of providing a health and safety consultant to advise and bring work practices up to standard.
- Possible prosecution.

Solutions
- Avoid storage of heavy or awkward items on high shelves (ie above shoulder height).
- Break down loads into smaller components that can be handled safely.
- Moving and handling training given to all workers, including volunteers, and repeated regularly.
- Effective accident reporting procedure.
- Follow up for workers off sick to establish if absence was work related.
- Consider fitness and capabilities of worker.

Notes
1   The back injury to the original worker should indicate a possible problem and required investigation to establish if the cause was work related.

Case study 33: Transporting a wheelchair user by car

Transporting someone using a wheelchair requires the volunteer to transport the wheelchair in their car. The wheelchair is of a standard design, manually operated and has large rear wheels and leg supports.

Hazards
- Lifting the wheelchair.
- Handling the wheelchair into a confined space.
- Heavy object in rear of vehicle.
- Lack of equipment restraints while driving.

Harm
- Injury to the volunteer from lifting the wheelchair.
- Increased risk of injury due to confined space – bending and twisting.
- Increased risk of injury on impact in an accident, due to risk of the wheelchair being thrown forward onto the passengers or driver.

Solutions
- Carry out a risk assessment of the moving and handling task.
- Agree the method for lifting the wheelchair, ie remove items that are easily detachable (like leg rests) and ensure the brakes are applied.
- Ensure the volunteer is competent at using the method or provide training.
- Ensure the wheelchair is stored securely to prevent movement or displacement.

Case study 34: Emptying boxes

The IT department had problems due to repetitive lifting of computer screens in and out of their packing boxes several times for various set up and operational reasons before installing them at workstations. Unsurprisingly, the people doing this work complained of backache.

Hazards
- Poor posture (bending, twisting, pulling etc).
- Moving and handling.

Harm
- Back injuries.
- Sickness absence.

Solutions
- Working with the supplier to eliminate two of the reasons for lifting the screens in and out of their boxes.
- Eliminating the final awkward lift by cutting off the box (using a safety knife) before the screen is removed rather than afterwards – this suggestion came from a worker.
- Moving and handling risk assessment.
- Training in correct moving and handling techniques.

Case study 35: Transferring a patient

This is a highly specialised activity requiring a specialised risk assessment. The risk assessment **must only** be carried out by a competent person, ie someone who has received proper, recognised training and/or has qualifications in this area. The assessment should form part of the patient's care plan.

A highly dependent patient (ie unable to help themselves), with complex medical needs (eg in-situ catheter and on steroid medication), wants to be transferred from his bed to the armchair.

Hazards
- Moving and handling a person.

Harm
- Back ache and/or other upper limb disorders to workers.
- Injuries to patient – steroids tend to make the skin very thin and easy to tear.
- Displacement of catheter.
- Dropping patient.

Solutions
- Risk assessment of transfer activity.
- Use moving and handling aids, eg overhead or mobile hoists (or floor turntable if the patient is able to support themselves during standing) – may need a sliding sheet to pull patient up the bed in order to position hoist sling.
- Pre-plan layout to put chair in best position to transfer patient.
- Get assistance from another worker if patient is large and/or likely to resist, flail around etc.
- Specific worker training in the correct techniques to move or transfer patients – these should be included in the patient's care plan.

Case study 36: Sheep shearing

A charity concerned with saving and maintaining rare animal breeds needs to carry out annual shearing of its flock of sheep.

Hazards
- Heavy, awkward and uncooperative loads.
- Unpredictable behaviour and movement of sheep during shearing.
- Static support of sheep's weight during shearing process.
- Repetitive activities.
- Long duration.
- Poor working posture – bending and twisting.
- Shear cables.
- Possible inexperience of workers.

Harm
- Back injuries.
- Infections.

Solutions
- Trained **and** experienced shearers.
- Regular rest and recovery breaks – avoid productivity targets and associated bonuses.
- Refreshments.
- Hygiene facilities, eg for hand washing.

Figure 9 Moving and handling flow chart

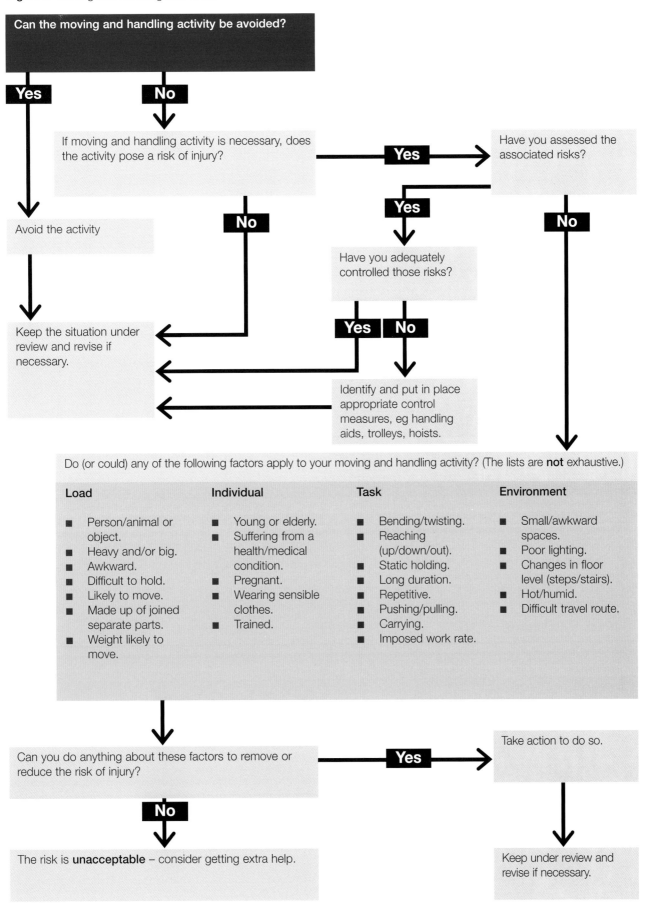

Can the moving and handling activity be avoided?

Yes

No

If moving and handling activity is necessary, does the activity pose a risk of injury?

Yes → Have you assessed the associated risks?

Avoid the activity

No

Yes

No

Have you adequately controlled those risks?

Keep the situation under review and revise if necessary.

Yes **No**

Identify and put in place appropriate control measures, eg handling aids, trolleys, hoists.

Do (or could) any of the following factors apply to your moving and handling activity? (The lists are **not** exhaustive.)

Load

- Person/animal or object.
- Heavy and/or big.
- Awkward.
- Difficult to hold.
- Likely to move.
- Made up of joined separate parts.
- Weight likely to move.

Individual

- Young or elderly.
- Suffering from a health/medical condition.
- Pregnant.
- Wearing sensible clothes.
- Trained.

Task

- Bending/twisting.
- Reaching (up/down/out).
- Static holding.
- Long duration.
- Repetitive.
- Pushing/pulling.
- Carrying.
- Imposed work rate.

Environment

- Small/awkward spaces.
- Poor lighting.
- Changes in floor level (steps/stairs).
- Hot/humid.
- Difficult travel route.

Can you do anything about these factors to remove or reduce the risk of injury?

Yes → Take action to do so.

No

The risk is **unacceptable** – consider getting extra help.

Keep under review and revise if necessary.

Table 10 Management checklist: Moving and handling

Checkpoints	Yes, No or N/A	Action required	
		By whom?	By when?
Risk assessment			
Can the moving and handling activity be avoided?			
Have you identified activities which might need specialist help to carry out risk assessments and provide training, eg: ■ moving and handling people using specialist equipment; ■ moving heavy and bulky objects in a warehouse; ■ moving and handling furniture; ■ use of specialist equipment, eg fork-lift trucks, hoists?			
Where the moving and handling activity cannot be avoided, have all workers been given instruction and training to do this safely?			
Have risk assessments been carried out and are all workers aware of safe handling practices?			
Assess the task			
Is the load heavy, bulky, unwieldy, fragile, people, animals, unpredictable?			
Is the individual trained and physically capable (age, gender, height)? Do they have any medical considerations (eg history of back pain, pregnancy)?			
Does the task involve stooping, twisting, bending, carrying for long distances, repetitive movements or a long duration?			
Does the environment have uneven surfaces, confined spaces, poor lighting or excessively hot or cold temperatures?			

Table 10 Management checklist: Moving and handling (continued)

Checkpoints	Yes, No or N/A	Action required	
		By whom?	By when?
Consider ways of reducing the risks			
Arrange for deliveries to the point of use, eg to the first floor office instead of ground floor reception.			
Plan storage to avoid heavy objects on top shelves or on the floor, eg store at mid-body height.			
Breaking heavy loads into smaller loads, eg split boxes of stationery.			
Provide stepladders to reach high areas to avoid overstretching.			
Use equipment for inanimate loads, eg trolleys for post, hoists, lifts, mechanical stair climbers etc.			
Use of equipment for animate loads, eg mobile hoists, overhead tracking, sliding sheets, turntables, lifting cushions, hi-low beds.			
Work as teams – encourage workers to ask for help.			
Provide gloves to help get a more secure grip. Use safety boots to protect against dropping, eg bricks or other heavy items.			
Train workers in relevant lifting and handling techniques with regular refreshers.			
Record and report all accidents.			
Regularly review risk assessments, especially following an accident.			

Work-related stress

Why tackle stress?

151 Pressure is part and parcel of all work and helps to keep us motivated and productive. But **excessive** pressure can lead to **stress** – which undermines performance, is costly to employers, and can make people ill.

152 Do not be fooled into thinking that because you manage a charity or voluntary organisation, ie carry out 'good work', that work-related stress won't be a problem. In a way this may put additional pressure on workers who may feel they are letting the charity down. This is particularly true for workers in care organisations.

153 Work-related stress, depression or anxiety is the leading cause of working days lost through work-related injury or ill health, with an estimated 12.5 million days a year lost in 2003/04. Each reported case of stress leads to an average of 28.5 days lost. As an employer or manager, there are a number of simple things that you can do to manage the problem.

What you must do

154 As an employer, you have a 'duty of care' to protect the health, safety and welfare of all employees while at work. You also have to **assess the risks** arising from hazards at work, including work-related stress.

155 This need not be difficult. Tackling stress should include:

■ collecting a range of information on the current situation (such as sickness absence, staff turnover or by using worker surveys);
■ promoting active discussion with workers and their representatives to identify practical improvements;
■ agreeing and sharing an action plan with workers;
■ regularly reviewing the situation to ensure you continue to improve.

Causes of work-related stress

156 HSE has identified six key areas of work that, if not properly managed, are the main sources of work-related stress. These are:

■ **Demands:** such as workload, work patterns and the work environment.
■ **Control:** such as how much input the person has in the way they do their work.
■ **Support:** such as encouragement from line managers and colleagues, training and access to employee assistance programmes and/or occupational health services.
■ **Relationships:** such as avoiding conflict, and dealing with unacceptable behaviour fairly and consistently.
■ **Role:** such as ensuring workers understand their role and responsibilities within the organisation.
■ **Change:** such as how organisational change (large or small) is managed and communicated.

157 Some additional information that you may want to think about under each of these six main sources of work-related stress are given in paragraphs 158-182.

Demands

How much work is there?

158 Ensure there are sufficient resources to do the work allocated:

■ If there are insufficient resources, seek guidance from management about priorities.
■ Support your workers by helping them prioritise or renegotiate deadlines.
■ Cover workloads during workers absences.
■ Adjust work patterns to cope with peaks (this needs to be fair and agreed with workers).

159 If people are under-loaded, think about giving them more responsibility, but make sure that they have been adequately trained. Strike a balance between ensuring that workers are interested and busy, but not under-loaded, overloaded, or confused about the job. Develop personal work plans to ensure workers know what their job involves.

Are workers able to do the job?

160 Provide training and development:

- Train workers so they are able to do their jobs.
- Implement personal development/training plans which require individuals to identify development/training opportunities which can then be discussed with management.
- Devise systems to keep training records up to date to ensure workers are competent and comfortable in undertaking the core functions of their job.

Communication

161 Encourage workers to talk to you at an early stage if they feel they are unable to cope. Develop a system to notify workers of unplanned tight deadlines and any exceptional need to work long hours. Talk to your team regularly about what needs to be done. This can:

- help you understand the challenges the team are currently facing and any pressures they are under;
- find ways of sharing the work sensibly and agreeing the way forward with the team;
- gain team cohesion and commitment to the work you have planned – the team is likely to be more responsive if it understands what needs to happen and by when. Allocating more work to an already stretched team without explanation is unhelpful;
- ensure shift-work systems are agreed with workers and their representatives and that the shifts are fair in terms of workload;
- gain understanding and commitment to unplanned tight deadlines and any exceptional need for long hours;
- help you manage any unexpected absences or losses to the team – everyone knows the key stages of the project and what each other's role is;
- lead by example.

How good is the work environment?

162 Have suitable, sufficient and up-to-date risk assessments to control hazards associated with the work environment. Ensure inside workplaces are pleasant and comfortable to work in and suitable for the work activities carried out there.

163 Change start and finish times to help workers cope with pressures external to the organisation (eg childcare, poor commuting routes).

164 Assess the risk of physical violence and verbal abuse. Take steps to deal with this in consultation with workers and others who can help (eg the police, charities). Provide training to help workers deal with and defuse difficult situations (eg difficult phone calls, aggressive members of the public).

Control

165 Enable workers to have their say:

- Give more control to workers by enabling them to plan their own work, make decisions about how that work should be completed and how problems should be tackled (eg through project meetings, one-to-one meetings, performance reviews etc).
- Allocate responsibility to teams to take projects forward:
  - discuss and define teams at the start of the project;
  - agree objectives and goals;
  - agree team roles;
  - agree timescales;
  - agree the provision of managerial support (eg through regular progress meetings).
- Talk about the way decisions are made within the unit – is there scope for more team involvement?

166 Make full use of workers' skills and abilities:

- Enrich jobs by ensuring that workers are able to use various skills to get tasks completed, and that workers can understand how their work fits into the wider aims of the department or organisation.
- Talk about the skills workers have and if they believe they are able to use them to good effect. How else would they like to use their skills?

How much supervision is actually needed?

167 Only monitor workers output if this is essential. Regular meetings with workers could be arranged to see how things are going. At these meetings managers could provide advice and support where necessary and ensure that workers are coping.

Support

168 A supportive environment is crucial. Workers need to know that managers will support them, even if things go wrong or if they find that they are unable to cope with added pressures. Do you:

- Give support and encouragement to workers, even when things go wrong?
- Encourage workers to share their concerns about work-related stress at an early stage?
- Hold regular liaison/team meetings to discuss unit pressures?
- Hold regular one-to-one meetings to talk about any emerging issues or pressures?
- Value diversity? Don't discriminate against people on grounds of race, sex or disability or other irrelevant reasons.
- Seek examples of how the team would like to, or have, received good support from managers or colleagues? Can these be adopted across the unit?
- Ask how workers would like to access managerial support ('open-door' policies, agreed times when managers are able to discuss emerging pressures etc)?

169 When you manage your team's time:

- encourage a healthy work–life balance;
- encourage workers to take their annual leave entitlement and their meal breaks;
- include 'work-related stress/emerging pressures' as a standing item of workers meetings and/or performance reviews; and
- introduce flexibility in work schedules (where possible) to enable workers to cope with domestic commitments.

170 How well do you listen? Do you:

- Listen to your workers and agree a course of action for tackling any problems? It is important for workers to feel that the contribution they make at work is valued.
- Involve your workers? They need to do their bit to identify problems and work towards agreed solutions.
- Talk about ways the organisation could provide support if someone is experiencing problems outside work.
- Disseminate information on other areas of support (human resources department, occupational health, trained counsellors, charities)?

171 How do you meet the needs of the team? Do you:

- Provide your workers with suitable and sufficient training to do their jobs?
- Give new workers a proper induction into your team and the organisation?
- Remember that people's skills and the way they approach the work will differ?
- Develop individual or unit training arrangements and refresher sessions to ensure training and competencies are up to date and appropriate for the core functions of their job?
- Offer training in basic counselling skills/access to counsellors?
- Ensure workers know how to prioritise, or how to seek help if they have conflicting priorities?
- Provide training on time management, prioritisation, assertiveness etc?

Relationships

172 When dealing with unacceptable behaviour:

- work in partnership with workers to ensure that bullying and harassment never emerge as an issue. One way of doing this is by having procedures in place, such as disciplinary and grievance procedures, to deal with instances of unacceptable behaviour;
- in consultation with workers and their representatives, draw up effective policies to reduce or eliminate harassment and bullying;
- agree and implement procedures to prevent (or quickly resolve) conflict at work, and communicate these to workers;
- agree and implement a confidential reporting system to enable the reporting of unacceptable behaviour;
- communicate the policies and make it clear that senior management fully support them; and
- communicate the consequences of breaching the policies.

173 Do you work for a caring organisation?

- Create a culture where team members trust each other and can be trusted themselves while they are at work.
- Encourage your workers to recognise the individual contributions of other team members and the benefits of the whole team pulling together.
- Encourage good communication and provide appropriate training to aid skill development (eg listening skills, confidence building).

174 How well do you build teams?

- Select or build teams that have the right blend of expertise and experience for new projects.
- Provide training to help workers deal with and defuse difficult situations.
- Discuss how individuals work together and how they can build positive relationships.
- Identify ways to celebrate success (eg informal lunches/wash-up meetings at the end of projects).

Role

175 Make sure workers are clear about their role:

- Make sure your workers have a clearly defined role, eg through a personal work plan so they understand exactly what their roles and responsibilities are.
- Encourage your workers to talk to you at an early stage if they are not clear about priorities or the nature of the task to be undertaken.
- Talk to all your workers regularly to make sure that they are clear about their current job, what it entails, what you expect of them and what they can expect from you.
- Hold team meetings to enable team members to clarify their role and discuss any possible role conflict.
- Display team/department targets and objectives to help clarify the role of the unit and the individual.

176 How well do you manage new recruits?

- Make sure that new workers receive a comprehensive induction into your organisation. If this is not arranged centrally, you should do it locally.
- If your organisation has gone through change, check with your team to make sure they understand their new roles and are comfortable with them.
- Develop suitable induction arrangements for new workers – make sure all team members understand the role and responsibilities of the new recruit.

177 Make sure workers understand what you expect from them:

- Agree specific standards of performance for jobs and individual tasks and review these periodically.
- Introduce personal work plans which are linked to the outputs of the department or organisation.
- Introduce or revise job descriptions to help ensure that the core functions and priorities of the post are clear.
- Hold regular one-to-one meetings to ensure that individuals are clear about their role and know what is planned for the coming months.

Change

178 Make sure workers understand the reasons for change:

- Ensure all workers are aware of why the change is happening – agree and implement a system for doing this.
- Explain what the organisation wants to achieve and why it is essential that the change takes place; explain the timetable for action and what the first steps are going to be. Talk about what the change will mean in terms of day-to-day activity and discuss whether there are any new training needs.
- Communicate new developments quickly to avoid the spread of rumours in the organisation. If the organisation is planning a major change, your workers are likely to be discussing job security, whether they will need to relocate, and whether their terms and conditions will change.
- Face-to-face communication is generally best so that people have the opportunity to ask questions and say what they feel, but any means (eg paper, electronic) would be helpful.
- Have an 'open-door' policy where workers can talk to you about their concerns or any suggestions they have for improving the way change is managed.

179 Involve workers in changes:

- Provide a confidential system to enable workers to comment and ask questions before, during and after the change.
- Involve workers in discussions about how jobs might be developed and changed and in generating ways of solving problems.
- Supporting your workers is essential during a change.
- Involve workers in discussions about how jobs might be developed and changed.
- Have an 'open-door' policy to help workers who want to talk to their managers about their concerns.

180 Help workers adversely affected by change:

- Ensure that workers are aware of the impact of the change on their jobs.
- Help workers who are to be made redundant by the change by giving them the skills they need to find a new job, for example by helping them to write a CV and prepare for interviews.
- After the change think about revising work objectives to avoid role conflict and role ambiguity.
- Revise your risk assessment/action plans to see if any changes, for example a decrease in worker numbers, have resulted in increased hazards to remaining workers.
- Remember that social changes (eg if workers are now working with a completely different group of people) may have more of an impact on the individual than technological or geographical changes.

181 The HSE Management Standards approach provides a framework and process against which to develop an effective risk assessment, and is supported by a comprehensive toolkit designed to help organisations measure and improve their performance in tackling stress.

182 The Management Standards are available in full, with the toolkit, at www.hse.gov.uk/stress/standards. Paragraphs 183-187 provide a summary of the approach.

Assess whether stress is a problem in your workplace

183 There are a number of ways to identify the causes of stress in your workplace:

- **Using existing information** to see how your organisation shapes up. Sickness absence, staff turnover data, team and/or one-to-one meetings could help, as could any surveys, eg worker satisfaction surveys that you may have undertaken to get the views of workers.
- **Conducting a stress survey** of workers can be useful and can provide an indication of potential problem areas.
- **Discussion with employees** is an effective way of assessing stressors in your workplace and identifying locally relevant problems and solutions.

184 Whichever technique you use to assess stress, it is important that you talk to, and involve, your workers and their representatives.

Develop solutions

185 Finding solutions is often the most difficult part of tackling the possible causes of work-related stress. Each workplace and each worker is different, meaning that it is not possible to provide one set of solutions for all circumstances. Case studies of solutions that have worked for other organisations are available on HSE's Stress web pages and in the *Real solutions, real people* resource pack. Some basic improvements you can make are suggested paragraphs 186-187.

186 Your workers are likely to be the best source of practical solutions to problems affecting them. A representative **focus group** of 6-10 workers is an effective way of exploring problems and discussing solutions. Alternatively, an existing group (such as a worker or team meeting) may be appropriate.

187 The most important thing is that you continue to **talk to workers** to identify issues that affect them at work and to discuss practical solutions. Record what you decide to do in an action plan, share it with workers and stick to it. It is important that your **action plan** provides for a review of your risk assessment, to check the effectiveness of your actions and to ensure your organisation continues to improve the way it manages work-related stress.

Further information

HSE Management Standards web pages: www.hse.gov.uk/stress/standards

Real solutions, real people: A managers' guide to tackling work-related stress HSE Books 2003 ISBN 0 7176 2767 5

Working together to reduce stress at work: A guide for employees Leaflet MISC686 International Stress Management Association 2005 (single copy free or priced packs of 15 ISBN 0 7176 6122 9)

Making the stress Management Standards work: How to apply the Standards in your workplace Leaflet MISC714 International Stress Management Association 2005 (single copy free or priced packs of 15 ISBN 0 7176 6157 1)

Case study 37: Tasks beyond workers capabilities

A volunteer office worker in a charity providing assistance to elderly people worked two days a week. The office manager asked her if she would like to work on reception and the volunteer readily agreed. The charity made sure that training was given and were careful to supervise the volunteer, encouraging her to ask for help whenever needed. The office manager was aware that the volunteer had suffered from a period of stress-related illness, which had caused her to resign from her job as a teacher. Very soon after this new working arrangement, the volunteer began to take frequent sickness absences and when she discussed this with the office manager it became clear that she was not happy with the responsibility of the reception work – especially when clients became rude or aggressive or if they were in obvious distress themselves. While the manager was sympathetic to this she could not understand why it should cause a problem since the volunteer only worked two days a week and had the rest of the week to recover. The volunteer did not want to do reception work any more but was told that there was currently no other work available.

Hazards
- Dealing with difficult and/or emotional people.
- Work more demanding than the current capability of the worker.
- Lack of control over the work.

Harm
- Stress.
- Sickness absence.
- Extra workload to be picked up by other workers.
- Loss of volunteer and/or goodwill.

Solutions
- Match the work activity to the capabilities of the worker.
- Staff support, eg counselling, occupational health visits.
- Proactive rehabilitation and return-to-work policies and procedures in place.

Case study 38: Workload

The local coffee shop is run by a voluntary organisation that employs a co-ordinator; all the other people involved are volunteers. The co-ordinator has to meet the agreed targets for the department, ensure the expectations of the customers are met and support the volunteers. Recently the co-ordinator has been working long hours covering for absence due to vacancies and sickness. She is experiencing headaches, fatigue, difficulty concentrating and loss of confidence.

Hazards
- Lack of control over work tasks and load.
- Unrealistic targets.
- Long hours of work.
- Under staffing.

Harm
- Stress.
- General ill health.
- Fatigue.
- Loss of co-ordinator (temporary or permanent) and associated costs.
- Ineffective supervision of volunteers.
- Increased risk of accidents.

Solutions
- Identify actual causes of the stress.
- Review the co-ordinator's role.
- Support the co-ordinator and review the worker support systems – ie, supervision, peer review, counselling.
- Organise for a deputy or delegation of responsibility.
- Ensure those with responsibility (steering committees, trustees etc) are fully involved and engaged in seeking solutions.
- Produce and agree a work plan and review this at regular intervals.
- Arrange a back-up worker rota to cover in emergencies and unexpected absences.

Notes
1   Many people working in voluntary organisations show considerable commitment and passion, for many this goes beyond the 'normal call of duty'. Recognise that people can be placed in highly stressful situations, and therefore effective management is essential.

Case study 39: Work environment

The data input department of a charity was moved into a temporary basement office while some essential building work was carried out to their own office. The temporary office was too small, badly decorated, poorly lit and ventilated and next to the lift motor room. Due to unexpected problems, the senior management team agreed to make the temporary office arrangements permanent.

Hazards
- Poor and unhealthy environmental conditions in the office.

Harm
- Stress.
- Ill health.
- Reduced productivity.
- Inaccurate data input.
- Increased sickness absence.
- Breakdown in worker relations.

Solutions
- Involve the workers in the decisions that directly affect them at work.
- Keep the workers informed of decisions made – provide clear accurate information.
- Rearrange working hours to reduce the number of workers at any one time.
- Look for other more suitable or additional office space.
- Redecorate the office.
- Provide more effective lighting and ventilation.
- Soundproof the lift motor room walls to reduce noise transfer.
- Consider the office layout to maximise available space and its use.

Notes
1 Several workers displaying the signs and symptoms of stress at the same time is a good indication that the cause may be poor environmental factors within their workplace, ie there is a common cause and a collective (not individual) adverse reaction.

Figure 10 Stress at work flow chart

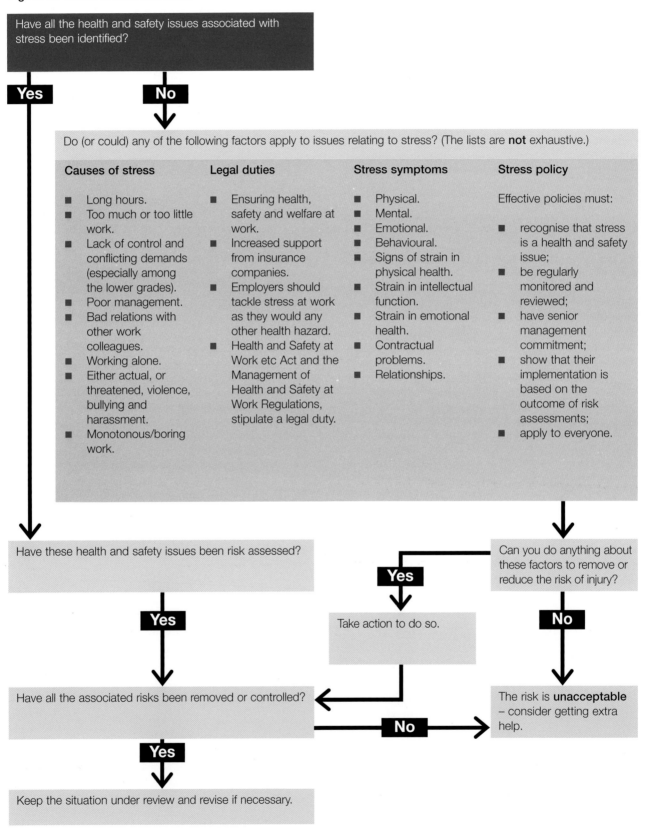

Have all the health and safety issues associated with stress been identified?

Yes   **No**

Do (or could) any of the following factors apply to issues relating to stress? (The lists are **not** exhaustive.)

Causes of stress

- Long hours.
- Too much or too little work.
- Lack of control and conflicting demands (especially among the lower grades).
- Poor management.
- Bad relations with other work colleagues.
- Working alone.
- Either actual, or threatened, violence, bullying and harassment.
- Monotonous/boring work.

Legal duties

- Ensuring health, safety and welfare at work.
- Increased support from insurance companies.
- Employers should tackle stress at work as they would any other health hazard.
- Health and Safety at Work etc Act and the Management of Health and Safety at Work Regulations, stipulate a legal duty.

Stress symptoms

- Physical.
- Mental.
- Emotional.
- Behavioural.
- Signs of strain in physical health.
- Strain in intellectual function.
- Strain in emotional health.
- Contractual problems.
- Relationships.

Stress policy

Effective policies must:

- recognise that stress is a health and safety issue;
- be regularly monitored and reviewed;
- have senior management commitment;
- show that their implementation is based on the outcome of risk assessments;
- apply to everyone.

Have these health and safety issues been risk assessed?

Can you do anything about these factors to remove or reduce the risk of injury?

Yes

Take action to do so.

Yes

No

Have all the associated risks been removed or controlled?

No

The risk is **unacceptable** – consider getting extra help.

Yes

Keep the situation under review and revise if necessary.

Table 11 Management checklist: Work-related stress – are we doing enough?

Checkpoints	Yes, No or N/A	Action required	
		By whom?	By when?
Organisational commitment			
Is there a member of staff responsible for managing stress/staff well-being?			
Are your trade unions signed up and involved?			
Are managers aware of their day-to-day responsibility to manage stress/staff well-being?			
Understanding the causes			
Do you understand what the key causes of work-related stress are?			
Are managers and staff aware of the issues that could be affecting them?			
Gathering the right information			
Does your organisation collect data on sickness absence and its causes?			
Do you monitor staff turnover and/or conduct exit interviews?			
Does your organisation conduct a staff survey to find out how employees feel about their jobs?			
Tackling problems at source			
Does your organisation take action to resolve issues that are affecting staff well-being?			
Do you take action to resolve issues in teams or at sites where there appear to be problems?			
Do you involve employees and their representatives in planning actions?			
Recording and monitoring			
Do you have an action plan for stress/staff well-being in place?			
Is this plan shared with all employees and their representatives?			
Do you check that the plan is being implemented and report to senior management?			
Do you review your risk assessment at least once every two years?			
Dealing with individual concerns			
Do you conduct return-to-work interviews and make appropriate adjustments following stress-related absences?			
Do all employees know how to use your procedures for dealing with bullying and harassment?			

Violence at work

188 Violence at work is becoming an increasingly important health and safety issue. While violence or aggression can occur in any work situation, there are certain jobs where it is more common. These jobs tend to be in teaching, nursing and where workers have to work with the public, eg social workers, shop workers. High-risk jobs also include caring for people with challenging behaviour.

189 The term 'violence at work' includes any form of threat, assault or abuse (whether physical and/or verbal) to a worker while they are at work. Physical attacks are obviously dangerous, but serious or persistent verbal abuse or threats can be a significant problem too, as they can damage workers' health through anxiety and stress.

190 The key to managing violence at work is to identify that there is a problem, then carry out a risk assessment to find out the causes and necessary control measures. Confirming that there is a problem with violence may be difficult if workers feel embarrassed about reporting such incidents.

191 There is a lot of similarity between causes and control of work-related violence and work-related stress – it is recommended that the *Stress at work* chapter is read in conjunction with this chapter.

Causes of violence

192 There are several known reasons why people become aggressive or violent. These are:

■ frustration:
   — lack of control over work;
   — inability to do something;
   — inaccurate or unclear information;
   — conflicting demands or instructions;
   — perceived unfair treatment;
■ extreme negative emotions:
   — bereavement or other significant loss;
   — depression;
   — anxiety/worry;
■ feeling threatened or afraid:
   — physical, eg bullying, harassment;
   — mental, eg emotional blackmail, manipulation;
■ substance abuse or use:
   — drugs, alcohol or caffiene;
   — inadvertent or unknown side effects of medications;
■ mental illness or injury:
   — challenging behaviour;

■ personal tolerances and 'comfort zones':
   — personal space invasion;
   — personalities, eg volatile, confrontational;
■ contributory factors:
   — worker's own body language;
   — workplace layout, eg two chairs placed on opposite sides of a desk can come across as confrontational;
   — colours – certain colours can increase aggressive responses, eg red.

Warning signs

193 Very few violent incidents are spontaneous; in nearly all cases there will be warning signs that a person is becoming increasingly aggressive and may become violent. The trick is to be able to recognise these warning signs and act on them before something serious occurs.

194 Common warning signs are:

■ behavioural changes:
   — increased body tension, agitation, excitability;
   — withdrawal;
   — lack of concentration;
   — violent hallucinations or delusions;
■ known histories:
   — mental illness or injury;
   — substance abuse or use;
   — medication side effects;
   — known exposure to extreme negative emotions;
■ high-risk situations:
   — inner cities;
   — high crime rate areas;
   — work involving handling money or valuables;
   — lone working;
   — public services, especially when they go wrong.

195 Behavioural changes usually follow a set pattern:

■ agitation, eg wringing hands, pacing, fidgeting;
■ disruption, eg tapping or clicking fingers, making a noise;
■ destruction, eg damage to objects and furniture;
■ threat of physical harm, eg specific threats of injury;
■ physical harm.

196 The earlier in this sequence that the potential for violence is recognised, the more effective the control measures will be. Once a person reaches the final stage they will be very difficult if not impossible to stop.

Control measures

197 To some extent the control measures will depend on the person involved and the reasons why they have become aggressive or violent. There are, however, some basic precautions that can be followed:

■ provide clear, understandable, accurate communication and information;
■ avoid lone working in situations of high or unknown risk;
■ security:
— avoid becoming trapped or cornered – always keep a clear access to the door;
— check out unknown locations before visiting;
— provide personal alarms;
— provide panic buttons, eg on reception desks to alert others of a problem – there must be a procedure in place for someone to respond if the panic alarm is used;
— use coded and other secure entrances;
— secure storage of highly sought-after items, eg drugs, money;
— install wide/high counters, CCTV and other premises security measures;
■ have contact procedures;
■ organisation of work:
— make high-risk appointments during the day, avoid non-routine hours where possible;
— frequently change banking routines for money;
— request donations as cheques rather than cash;
— environmental factors:
— good lighting and decoration – use calming, soothing natural colours;
— comfortable and clean;
— private;
— not overcrowded;
— remove potential missiles from high-risk situations, eg waste bins, fire extinguishers;
■ diffusion:
— stay calm and in control;
— control own body language;
— talk/communicate;
— establish facts and the reasons for the behaviour;
— keep a safe distance;
— always be able to escape;
— explain everything that is going on;
■ implement policies and procedures for calling for assistance:
— provide clear guidance on what behaviour will and will not be tolerated or accepted – the NHS has a 'zero tolerance' to violence towards its workers;

— have procedures for dealing with challenging behaviour where the violence may be accidental or inadvertent (ie no control over actions or responses);
— have a policy on restraint, ie are restraints permitted and if so, what type and when. Clear procedures are required to prevent inadvertent abuse.

After an aggressive or violent incident

198 If a worker experiences an aggressive or violent attack, even if it is verbal, it is very important that the incident is formally reported and the worker given staff support. The staff support may include any or all of the following:

■ debriefing and establishing the facts;
■ counselling – arrangements should be private and confidential;
■ time off to recover from the incident and to attend any medical or counselling appointments;
■ legal help if prosecutions are taken.

Further information

Preventing violence to retail staff HSG133 HSE Books 1995 ISBN 0 7176 0891 3

Work-related violence: Case studies – Managing the risk in smaller businesses HSG229 HSE Books 2002 ISBN 0 7176 2358 0

Violence and aggression to staff in health services: Guidance on assessment and management HSE Books 1997 ISBN 0 7176 1466 2

Violence in the education sector HSE Books 1997 ISBN 0 7176 1293 7

Violence at work: A guide for employers Leaflet INDG69(rev) HSE Books 1996 (single copy free or priced packs of 10 ISBN 0 7176 1271 6)

A series of real-life case studies offering practical ways to reduce the threat of violence to lone workers are available on HSE's website (www.hse.gov.uk/violence).

Case study 40: Inadvertent violence to workers

A volunteer classroom assistant in a special needs school receives several hard punches and slaps, seemingly without provocation, while working with a child.

Hazards
- Violent behaviour.
- Unpredictable behaviour patterns of pupils.

Harm
- Personal injury to the staff member.
- Increased risk of occupational stress.
- Staff member requires time to recover.
- Reluctance to work with the child.

Solutions
- Provide staff training in 'positive intervention' techniques and keeping themselves safe.
- Record each incident as fully and soon as possible.
- Review admissions criteria and referrals policy.
- Review the incident circumstances to identify triggers to this behaviour and any further control measures needed.
- Review and (if necessary) update the child's support plan.
- Ensure workers are told about any new guidelines.
- Review regularly and invite feedback.

Notes
1   Aggression or violence may be intentional or unintentional and may be unpredictable.
2   Positive interventions are actions taken to deal with potentially aggressive or violent situations and can range from simply distracting a child through to competent physical restraint.
3   The organisation must have a restraint policy that clearly defines when and how physical restraints may used.

Case study 41: Telephone operator dealing with verbal abuse

A caller makes repeated calls following changes to the service they have received. The calls become increasingly abusive and personal.

Hazards
- Abuse.
- Threats.

Harm
- Intimidation and fear.
- Stress.
- Severe traumatic reactions.
- Worker sickness absence.
- Low morale and demotivation of individuals and teams.
- Reduction in productivity.

Solutions
- Give operators information about service changes with pre-planned answers.
- Guidance and training for managing abusive calls including how to end these calls.
- Staff support programme that includes debriefing, counselling and recovery time.
- Report, record and investigate all incidents – review and revise procedures accordingly.

Notes
1   Callers may be able to get details on individual workers via the organisation's website and publicity materials.
2   Callers may be skilled enough to get personal information from the operator or their colleagues without them being aware of it.

Case study 42: Theft from a charity shop

Two people enter the shop; one distracts the shop worker while the other steals items. A work colleague intervenes to stop the theft.

Hazards
- Verbal aggression (to shop workers and/or customers).
- Physical assault (to shop workers and/or customers).

Harm
- Injury (to shop workers and/or customers).
- Traumatic stress reaction (to shop workers and/or customers).
- Sickness absence.
- Property damage.
- Loss of revenue.

Solutions
- Design the shop front to reduce the opportunities for theft, ie place the till away from the door.
- Train workers in personal safety and dealing with difficult people.
- Provide clear instruction for workers to manage situations, eg don't put yourself in danger and report to the police.
- Provide worker support programmes such as telephone helplines and face-to-face counselling.
- Join a local 'shop watch' scheme – see Notes below.

Notes
1 'Shop watch' is like a 'neighbourhood watch' scheme where local shops pass on and share information about suspicious people and adverse events.

Case study 43: Drug drop-in centre

This 'drop-in' centre for drug users is situated in a large city. It is run by a charity and employs seven employees and 12 volunteers. The centre provides drug users, their friends and families with help and advice on drug-related problems, and also provides professional counselling. Aggressive and violent situations are common.

Hazards
- Unpredictable behaviour of clients.

Harm
- Assault leading to personal injuries and/or property damage.
- Verbal abuse from clients to workers and each other.

Solutions
- Ensure effective emergency procedures are in place, eg panic alarms with links to identified other workers and/or the police in all client areas.
- Provide effective means of security (such as CCTV, intruder alarms) to protect client records.
- Provide clear and up-to-date information to clients.
- Provide effective training and information:
  - workers adopt a non-confrontational and non-judgemental approach to clients;
  - workers are trained to avoid being patronising, and to help create an equal balance of power between workers and clients;
  - workers are familiar with the control measures in place to protect them.
- Good design and layout:
  - clearly displayed notices stating that there is a 'zero tolerance' approach to violence and aggression;
  - light, spacious, airy and well-decorated public and working areas to give calming and welcoming effect;
  - reception desk to provide a central control point from which all client accessible areas can be supervised;
  - counselling rooms provide privacy but are within hearing distance of the reception and have panic alarms fitted;
  - worker offices are located out of client sight and open plan to allow workers to see each other.
- Good job design:
  - good appointment system;
  - continuous staffing of reception;
  - procedures are in place to follow up calls for assistance when the panic alarms are used.

Figure 11 Violence at work flow chart

If the work activity does or could involve exposure to aggression or violence, have you assessed and removed or controlled the associated risks?

Yes → Keep under review and revise as necessary.

No ↓

Consider any of the following factors that apply. (The lists are **not** exhaustive).

Causes

- Frustration, eg:
  - lack of or confusing information;
  - ability to do job.
- Extreme negative emotions, eg:
  - bereavement;
  - anxiety.
- Threatening and/or intimidating behaviour, eg:
  - bullying, harassment.
- Substance abuse, eg:
  - alcohol;
  - drugs.
- Mental illness or injury.
- Violation of personal tolerances and comfort zones.
- Aggressive/volatile personalities.

Other factors

- Hostile or threatening environments, eg:
  - dark;
  - cramped;
  - poor decoration.
- Known high risks, eg:
  - locations:
    - high crime rates;
    - poorly lit;
    - isolated;
  - handling money;
  - handling or storage of drugs;
  - dealing with the public/people.

Controls

- Accurate, clear information.
- Avoid lone working.
- Effective security measures.
- Physical barriers (if appropriate).
- Contact procedures for lone working.
- Work organisation to avoid high-risk situations.
- Non-hostile or threatening environmental factors.
- Diffusion of aggressive or violent situations.
- Clear policies, procedures.

↓

Can you do anything about them?

Yes → Take action to do so. → **Yes** → Keep under review and revise as necessary.

No → Risks may be **unacceptable** – consider getting extra help.

Table 12 Manager's checklist: Violence at work

Checkpoints	Yes, No or N/A	Action required	
		By whom?	By when?
Policy			
Is there a clear policy statement that defines acceptable behaviour standards towards workers with regard to aggression and violence (eg 'zero tolerance')?			
Assess the risks			
Have you identified any work activities where workers are likely to come across aggressive or violent behaviour, eg: ■ from past incident reports; ■ where there are lone workers; ■ where money or drugs are handled; ■ where clients themselves may already be prone to violent and/or unpredictable behaviour patterns; or ■ where requests for service may be refused?			
Reporting and investigating incidents			
Where the risk of violence has been identified, have workers been trained to confidently manage the situation?			
Are all incidents reported, recorded and investigated?			
Does this include verbal as well as physical aggression?			
If an incident does occur, is this investigated fully by management and support given to any workers affected?			
Where clients come into the workplace, provide a welcoming environment			
Are they given reasons for unavoidable delays?			
Are all efforts made to keep to appointment times?			
Is the waiting area comfortable?			
Are waiting times kept to a minimum?			
Are reception staff trained to notice early warning signs and defuse aggressive situations?			
Are there tried and tested ways of dealing with an emergency, eg use of panic buttons, backed up by response from colleagues?			
Are clients made aware that aggressive behaviour will not be tolerated and will be followed up by management or legal action?			

Table 12 Manager's checklist: Violence at work (continued)

Checkpoints	Yes, No or N/A	Action required	
		By whom?	By when?
Make sure control measures are in place to protect workers from violence			
Are work and public areas physically separated by design?			
Are reception areas carefully laid out to avoid heavy items that could be used as weapons? Provide magazines, drinking water etc.			
Are premises well lit?			
Do you monitor the safety and whereabouts of lone workers?			
Do you avoid situations where workers might be at risk?			
Do you have effective security arrangements?			

Work equipment

199 Every work activity will involve work equipment of some kind. Work equipment can be defined as any piece of machinery, tool, plant or other item needed for a worker to carry out their job.

200 By implication this is a very large area of health and safety and covers many different items and hazards. This chapter will look at the main hazards associated with work equipment and consider electrical equipment, lifting equipment and display screen equipment (computers etc) specifically.

201 Because of the range of equipment available, there are a lot of laws covering them. The main ones are:

- the Provision and Use of Work Equipment Regulations 1998 (PUWER) apply to all work equipment generally;
- the Electricity at Work Regulations 1989 apply to electrical equipment and work with electricity;
- the Lifting Operations and Lifting Equipment Regulations 1998 (LOLER) apply to all lifting equipment;
- the Health and Safety (Display Screen Equipment) Regulations 1992 (DSE Regulations) apply to all display screen equipment, not just computers;
- the Control of Noise at Work Regulations 2005 apply to all work activities where noise levels could cause hearing damage or loss;
- the Control of Vibration at Work Regulations 2005 apply to all work activities where there is a risk of injury caused by vibration.

Hazards associated with work equipment

202 The hazards and necessary control measures associated with work equipment will depend on the type of equipment in question. For example, the hazard associated with ladders is falling, while the hazard associated with a guillotine is contact with a sharp blade.

203 Some common hazards you may need to consider are listed below:

- electrocution or electric shock;
- contact with moving parts;
- parts breaking up and being thrown out;
- hot/cold parts;
- sharp surfaces or blades;
- entrapment;
- entanglement;
- explosion;
- falls from height;
- noise;
- vibration – hand-arm and/or whole-body vibration;
- fire.

Electrical equipment

204 The dangers associated with electricity, such as electric shock, electrocution and fire, are well known. There are three basic aspects you need to think about when looking at electrical health and safety:

- portable electrical equipment (anything that has a plug and that is capable of being moved);
- the electrical wiring systems within buildings;
- work on live electrical equipment.

Portable electrical equipment

205 Many work activities will involve the use of portable electrical equipment and you will need to ensure that your workers know how to use the equipment safely. Some common safety measures include:

- Train your workers to carry out a quick visual check of cables and plugs before any electrical equipment is used – have a system in place for removing, reporting and dealing with faulty or defective equipment.
- Ensure plugs are fitted with the correct fuses. They will be specified in the equipment instruction manuals.
- Portable appliance testing (PAT) – the frequency is a matter of judgement and depends on the degree of use and working environment. Equipment that successfully passes the PAT testing should be clearly labelled as such, along with the date that the test was carried out. PAT testing should be carried out by people who have been trained and who are competent to do so.
- Provide residual circuit devices (RCDs) (also known as circuit breakers) to workers using electrical equipment outdoors where there is potential for exposure to water and/or to damage, eg lawn mowers, strimmers, hedge-cutters etc. RCDs should also be considered for workers working off site and/or where the condition of the wiring system is not known.
- Control the use of extension leads and stop them being plugged into each other. Wherever possible, provide additional sockets in the workplace.
- Avoid the use of multiple adaptors. Follow the general rule of 'one plug to one socket'.
- Encourage workers to switch off and unplug electrical equipment that is not in use, and at the end of the working day. Ensure equipment is unplugged by pulling the plug not the cable.
- Avoid electrical equipment coming into contact with water. Specialised electrical equipment, such as wet/dry vacuum cleaners, is available if identified as necessary in your risk assessments.

- Ensure carbon dioxide or other suitable fire extinguishers are available where electrical equipment is used. Never use a water (red label) fire extinguisher on electrical equipment.

Building wiring

206 It is recommend that the wiring systems in your workplace should be checked and certified by competent electricians every five years. More frequent checks may be necessary if the building is open to the public, the wiring is old or there has been any known damage such as damage caused by pests (eg rats, mice or squirrels) or by fire.

207 You may need to consider additional electrical earthing in certain circumstances, eg in kitchens when electrical equipment (eg a microwave) is placed and used on metal tables. Sinks and washbasins may also need earthing. Competent electrical contractors will be able to advise.

Live electrical work

208 Work on live electrical equipment or systems must be avoided whenever possible. If it is absolutely necessary, it must be carried out by a qualified and competent electrician (it is your responsibility to check and ensure this competency) and meet three criteria in the Electricity at Work Regulations:

- it is unreasonable for the electricity to be dead (ie, it is too disruptive/costly – you will have to be able to justify this decision);
- work activities should not be carried out near live electricity unless it is necessary and safe to do so;
- suitable precautions are taken to prevent injury.

Lifting equipment

209 Lifting equipment is any equipment designed to lift and/or move loads. Examples of lifting equipment include:

- passenger lifts;
- dumb waiters (eg as used in hotels for transferring food between the kitchen and restaurant);
- mobile hoists, including those used to transfer people;
- overhead tracking systems;
- cranes;
- pulley systems and other associated parts, eg slings, chains etc;
- minibus and lorry tail lifts;
- fork-lift trucks.

210 There are very strict controls over the use of lifting equipment and its associated parts, eg slings, chains etc. These controls include:

- planning work activities involving lifting equipment;
- ensuring the lifting equipment is:
  - suitable, strong and stable enough for the intended use;
  - positioned or installed to prevent the risk of injury, eg being hit by the load;
  - clearly marked with its safe load weights/limits;
- the regular and scheduled thorough examination and inspection of the lifting equipment, with reports.

Display screen equipment

211 Display screen equipment (DSE) is the term used to cover all visual display units (VDUs) and work equipment that has a screen displaying text, numbers or graphics. When working with display screen equipment there are actions that must be taken to ensure safety and comfort. Ensure that:

- risks have been assessed and reduced;
- all workstations meet the minimum requirements. This applies to screens, keyboards, desks, chairs, the work environment and software;
- work is planned so that there are breaks or changes of activity, with more frequent shorter breaks preferable to less frequent longer breaks;
- training and information is provided.

212 Employees who habitually work with DSE are entitled to ask for an eye test provided by their employer. DSE work does not cause eye or eyesight damage, but can cause temporary eyestrain or headaches. Voluntary workers who experience these symptoms may also find it helpful to get an eye test, as visually demanding work like using DSE can highlight pre-existing visual defects (eg short or long sight). Correcting such defects may enable them to work more comfortably.

Common control measures for work equipment

213 These include:

- planned preventative maintenance, ie regular checks and services to spot problems before they cause any harm – detailed records should be kept;
- competent maintenance staff, ie professional electricians for electrical work, CORGI registered workers for gas equipment etc;
- annual portable appliance testing (PAT) on electrical equipment;
- visual checks on cables and leads before using electrical equipment;
- minimising use of extension leads and multiple adaptors;
- use of RCDs to detect electrical current leakages;
- correct use of electrical fuses;
- restricting use to authorised, competent operators;
- detailed information, instructions and supervision;
- relevant training to develop skills and competency;
- automatic guards to prevent contact with dangerous parts;
- door locks, eg as on washing machines to stop the door from being opened during a cycle;
- pre-planning before any equipment is bought:
  - where it will be sited;
  - suitability for intended purpose;
  - who will use it – do they have any special needs, eg left-handed;
- fail-safe systems, where the machine always stops in a 'safe' condition in an emergency or non-routine event;
- obvious and easy-to-use emergency/stop controls. Think about access to these controls by left-handed operators (most machines etc are designed for right-handed use);
- personal protective equipment and clothing.

Further information

Safe use of work equipment. Provision and Use of Work Equipment Regulations 1998. Approved Code of Practice and guidance L22 (Second edition) HSE Books 1998 ISBN 0 7176 1626 6

Simple guide to the Provision and Use of Work Equipment Regulations 1998 Leaflet INDG291 HSE Books 1999 (single copy free or priced packs of 15 ISBN 0 7176 2429 3)

Using work equipment safely Leaflet INDG229(rev1) HSE Books 2002 (single copy free or priced packs of 10 ISBN 0 7176 2389 0)

Buying new machinery: A short guide to the law and some information on what to do for anyone buying new machinery for use at work Leaflet INDG271 HSE Books 1998 (single copy free or priced packs of 15 ISBN 0 7176 1559 6)

Work with display screen equipment. Health and Safety (Display Screen Equipment) Regulations 1992 as amended by the Health and Safety (Miscellaneous Amendments) Regulations 2002. Guidance on Regulations L26 (Second edition) HSE Books 2003 ISBN 0 7176 2582 6

The law on VDUs: An easy guide: Making sure your office complies with the Health and Safety (Display Screen Equipment) Regulations 1992 (as amended in 2002) HSG90 HSE Books 2003 ISBN 0 7176 2602 4

Working with VDUs Leaflet INDG36(rev2) HSE Books 2003 (single copy free or priced packs of 10 ISBN 0 7176 2222 3)

Simple guide to the Lifting Operations and Lifting Equipment Regulations 1998 Leaflet INDG290 HSE Books 1999 (single copy free or priced packs of 15 ISBN 0 7176 2430 7)

Memorandum of guidance on the Electricity at Work Regulations 1989. Guidance on Regulations HSR25 HSE Books 1989 ISBN 0 7176 1602 9

Electricity at work: Safe working practices HSG85 (Second edition) HSE Books 2003 ISBN 0 7176 2164 2

Electrical safety and you Leaflet INDG231 HSE Books 1996 (single copy free or priced packs of 15 ISBN 0 7176 1207 4)

Maintaining portable and transportable electrical equipment (Second edition) HSG107 HSE Books 2004 ISBN 0 7176 2805 1

Maintaining portable electrical equipment in offices and other low-risk environments Leaflet INDG236 HSE Books 1996 (single copy free or priced packs of 10 ISBN 0 7176 1272 4)

Safety in electrical testing at work: General guidance Leaflet INDG354 HSE Books 2002 (single copy free or priced packs of 5 ISBN 0 7176 2296 7)

Do you use a steam/water pressure cleaner? You could be in for a shock! Leaflet INDG68(rev) HSE Books 1997 (single copy free)

Noise at work: Guidance for employers on the Control of Noise at Work Regulations 2005 Leaflet INDG362(rev1) HSE Books 2005 (single copy free or priced packs of 10 ISBN 0 7176 6165 2)

Control the risks from hand-arm vibration: Advice for employers on the Control of Vibration at Work Regulations 2005 Leaflet INDG175(rev2) HSE Books 2005 (single copy free or priced packs of 10 ISBN 0 7176 6117 2)

Control back-pain risks from whole-body vibration: Advice for employers on the Control of Vibration at Work Regulations 2005 Leaflet INDG242(rev1) HSE Books 2005 (single copy free or priced packs of 10 ISBN 0 7176 6119 9)

Safe use of ladders and stepladders: An employers' guide Leaflet INDG402 HSE Books 2005 (single copy free or priced packs of 5 ISBN 0 7176 6105 9)

Case study 44: Second-hand electrical equipment

A charity accepts donations of second-hand electrical items and equipment for its own use and for resale.

Hazards
■ Condition and history (and therefore safety) of equipment may be unknown.

Harm
■ Electric shock.
■ Electrocution.
■ Fire.

Solutions
■ Visually check all cables and plugs for obvious defects and damage.
■ Get equipment thoroughly checked out and certified by a qualified and competent electrician.
■ Ensure any current British Standards and/or European restrictions or conditions are met.
■ Clearly mark equipment as second-hand.

Notes
1   Second-hand equipment is subject to the requirements of PUWER and the Electricity at Work Regulations.
2   Many charities do not have access to qualified and competent electricians, so will not sell on second-hand electrical items because of the potential liabilities involved if something goes wrong.
3   It is the charity's responsibility to ensure the electrician used is competent.

Case study 45: Computer work

Despite a charity having valid DSE risk assessments in place and workstations and associated equipment that generally met the legal requirements, the number of cases of repetitive strain injury (RSI) cases continued to increase.

Investigation revealed that the main cause was workers not taking sufficient breaks from screen work, despite saying the opposite (as they thought was expected of them). In most cases there wasn't anything to prevent them taking breaks as and when they wanted to, but they worked continuously because of their self-motivation to do the best for the charity. This 'overworking' and the resulting health problems meant the charity was losing their valuable input.

Hazards
■ Prolonged work periods at computer.
■ Insufficient rest and recovery periods.

Harm
■ RSI-associated injuries, with possible long-term/permanent disabilities.

Solutions
■ Provide a detailed training programme to explain the importance of breaks and potential consequences – input from RSI sufferers could add a realistic and personal message.
■ Train managers in their responsibilities to monitor and control workloads and deadlines to ensure workers do not feel pressured into long periods of computer work.
■ Review workloads in the areas where RSI is most frequent to remove or reduce the volume of work required.
■ Worker support, eg access to occupational health services and other help, training in awareness for self-recognition of early RSI signs.
■ Provide DSE rest break monitoring software.[Note 2]
■ Provide health monitoring or an occupational health programme.

Notes
1   Regular reviews of workloads are useful in ensuring that the work actually being carried out has some purpose and benefit – it highlights work that is no longer necessary or urgent.
2   This is software installed onto the computers of workers identified a being a high RSI risk and monitors the time a worker is using their computer keyboard and mouse. The system is usually set up to the individual needs and working patterns of the worker and can be instructed to warn the worker to take a break or to enforce a break, eg lock the keyboard and mouse until a preset break from the computer has been taken.
3   In a successful court case, an employer was found guilty of not enforcing rest breaks from computer work, despite the workers being able to take breaks whenever they wanted and being given training on the importance of taking them. The court held that the employer should have been more proactive in enforcing the breaks.

Case study 46: Purchasing new work equipment

An animal rescue and welfare sanctuary wants to upgrade its laundry facilities and is looking to replace its washing machines.

Hazards
- Location of washing machines – confined spaces.
- Style of washing machines, eg front or top loading – poor working posture.
- Location of associated chemicals and vicinity of chemical store – moving and handling heavy loads.
- Fast spinning drum – contact with moving parts.
- Poor environmental conditions, eg lighting, temperature and ventilation.
- Fire – poor cleaning and maintenance, eg of dust filters in the machines.
- Chemicals.
- Electricity.

Harm
- Musculoskeletal disorders from poor posture, ie bending, stooping, twisting and/or reaching and from moving and handling heavy loads.
- Injuries associated with contact with moving parts, electricity and fire.
- Ill health associated with:
  — exposure to chemicals;
  — poor environmental conditions.
- Damage to property and loss of service due to fire.

Solutions
- Pre-plan what you actually need and where it will be used very carefully – involve the workers who will be using the equipment.
- Buy from a reputable supplier and try to look at significant items of work equipment in other workplaces before you decide to buy – most charities are happy to share information on their experiences.
- Include the new washing machines in a planned preventative maintenance programme – if they are essential to your operation, consider a rapid-response call out and a 'repair or replace' agreement with the supplier or service company.
- Washing machines should be fitted with:
  — a door-lock system that prevents the door from being opened during a wash cycle when the machine is in use;
  — a fail-safe system that always stops the machine in a 'safe condition' in an emergency.
- Ensure there is sufficient room for easy access to any associated chemicals when they have to be replaced – try to plan the chemical store nearby and to allow delivery of the chemicals directly into the store area (to prevent extra moving and handling by your workers).
- Decide who will be using the washing machines and what training they will need.
- Ensure you have a copy of the instruction manual and any other relevant safety information provided by the manufacturer or supplier.
- Arrange for the manufacturer or supplier to provide on-site training on using the washing machines once they are installed.
- Ensure workers actually know how to use the washing machines safely and how to stop them in an emergency.

Notes
1 The intended use of the washing machines must be clearly defined – ie what do you want them to be able to do, eg hot disinfection washes, short economy washes, deal with soiled loads.

Case study 47: Vehicle tail lifts

A charity buys two old vans to transport boxes of emergency aid from their temporary warehouse to the airport.

Hazards
- Failure of lifting equipment:
  - age of vans;
  - unknown tail-lift maintenance history.

Harm
- Injuries to workers.
- Damage to vehicle.
- Damage to goods.

Solutions
- Request maintenance, service and thorough examination paperwork associated with the tail lift.
- Get the tail lift independently checked and certified by someone competent in that type of lifting equipment.
- Provide a detailed planned examination and testing programme.
- Ensure workers do not ride up and down on the lift plate with the loads.
- If workers have to ride on the tail lift, provide a supporting handrail.
- Ensure safe working loads are clearly marked and are not exceeded.
- Ensure the emergency stop control is obvious and easy to reach.
- Stack loads carefully and safely – avoid leaning or unstable loads.
- Train all workers on safe use of the tail lift, including remote operation, safe load limits and emergency controls.

Notes
1   These same principles of maintenance etc apply to all lifting equipment and its accessories, including cranes, mobile hoists or overhead tracking systems.

Case study 48: Crockery

A 17-year-old volunteer with learning difficulties was washing the crockery (teapot, cups, saucers, spoons) used by workers that day. A cup was accidentally broken and the volunteer cut herself on the broken pieces. The cut required stitches and an operation to repair nerves in her fingers. Her parents sued for compensation.

Hazards
- Sharp edges to broken pieces of crockery.
- Vulnerable worker, ie young person and who has learning difficulties – may be less aware of the hazards associated with broken crockery.

Harm
- Cut injuries affecting tendons and/or nerves.
- Costs associated with being sued.
- Damaged reputation/bad publicity.

Solutions
- Provide ongoing special one-to-one coaching with worker to reinforce dangers and controls.
- Carry out a 'young person' risk assessment[Note 2] for the intended work activities, including washing up – a copy of this risk assessment must be sent to the young worker's parents or guardian if the worker is a child, ie under 16 years of age.
- Replace the crockery with sturdy plastic mugs or disposable plastic cups and use teabags instead of a teapot to prevent the risk of injury.

Notes
1   Health and safety law requires a higher duty of care to workers who may be more vulnerable, ie who are young and/or who have any form of disability.
2   The Management of Health and Safety at Work Regulations 1999 require employers to carry out a risk assessment for all work activities undertaken by young people (16-18 years of age) and children (under 16 years old).

Case study 49: Noise and vibration

A self-employed building worker volunteers to dig up the concrete floor covering an important drain access point for a charity responsible for the upkeep of various properties and buildings. The concrete floor has to be dug up using a hired pneumatic hammer drill and the worker arranges to do the work one Sunday morning to minimise disruption and inconvenience.

Hazards
- Noise.
- Vibration.
- Dust.
- Lone working.
- Other work equipment, eg compressor unit for the compressed air.

Harm
- Hearing damage or loss.
- Injuries associated with exposure to vibration.
- Breathing problems from dust.
- Eye injuries from flying concrete chips.

Solutions
- Hire equipment that is suitable for the intended use and purpose.
- Ensure the worker is competent to use the equipment – ask for training or qualification certificates, professional memberships, past clients who have used the worker's services etc.
- Ensure equipment has been well maintained and if possible find out likely levels of noise and vibration exposure – ask to see records.
- Try to isolate the drilling work to avoid or reduce noise exposure to other workers or people who may be in the vicinity.
- Organise work to allow sufficient breaks to recover from noise and vibration exposure.
- Mark off the work area to avoid unwanted access or interruptions.
- Provide appropriate personal protective equipment (PPE), eg ear protection, face (nose/mouth) mask, eye protection.

Notes
1   It is the charity's responsibility to ensure that the worker is competent to use the work equipment and that the equipment hired is ultimately safe.
2   Any PPE provided must be suitable for the risks it is intended to control, ie ear protection must be suitable for pneumatic drill use, face masks must be suitable for preventing breathing in of dust etc.

Figure 12 Work equipment flow chart

Have you assessed and removed or controlled the risks associated with all your work equipment?

Yes

No

Consider any of the following factors that could apply. (The lists are not exhaustive.)

General hazards

- Moving parts:
  - entrapment;
  - entanglement;
  - impact;
  - expelled parts or contents.
- Electricity.
- Fire/explosion.
- Sharp parts.
- Hot/cold parts.

Electrical controls

- Keep electricity and water apart.
- Visual cable etc checks before use.
- PAT testing.
- Avoid extension leads/multiple adapters.
- Incorrect fuses.
- Circuit breakers.

General controls

- Suitable for intended use.
- Emergency and stop controls.
- Fail-safe systems.
- Alarms.
- Location/siting.
- Adequate lighting.
- Sufficient space.
- Guarding.
- Planned preventive maintenance.
- Training.
- Information and instructions.
- Restricted use.
- Personal protective equipment (PPE).

Lifting equipment

- Failure of load-bearing parts.
- Safe working load limits.
- Competent maintenance.
- Examination schedule.
- Thorough examinations – keep records.
- Training.
- Alarms.

Remember, lifting equipment includes:

- passenger lifts;
- mobile patient hoists;
- cranes;
- industrial hoists;
- vehicle tail lifts.

Noise

- Isolate machinery.
- Dampen noise.
- Exposure:
  - levels;
  - periods;
  - duration;
  - frequencies.
- Marked areas.
- Ear protection.
- Health checks.

Vibration

Hand-arm or whole-body vibration:

- dampen causes;
- exposure:
  - levels;
  - periods;
  - duration;
  - frequencies;
- health checks.

Take action to do so.

Yes

Can you do anything about them?

No

Keep under review and revise as necessary.

Risks may be **unacceptable** – consider getting extra help.

Figure 13 Display screen equipment flow chart

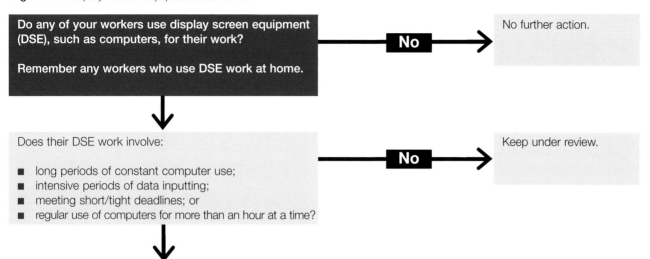

Do any of your workers use display screen equipment (DSE), such as computers, for their work?

Remember any workers who use DSE work at home.

No → No further action.

Does their DSE work involve:

- long periods of constant computer use;
- intensive periods of data inputting;
- meeting short/tight deadlines; or
- regular use of computers for more than an hour at a time?

No → Keep under review.

Make sure that the DSE workstation assessment covers the following factors:

Computer

- Clear screen images and characters.
- Stable, non-flicker images.
- Workers aware of how to change screen colour, text size and contrast/brightness.
- Screen can be swivelled and tilted.
- Screen correct height and viewing distance.
- Screen free from window glare or light reflection.
- Clearly contrasted keyboard keys.
- Keyboard can be tilted.
- Mouse is positioned close to worker.
- Suitable software for intended use.
- Following accessories provided as necessary:
  - wrist support;
  - mouse support;
  - foot rests;
  - document holder.

Chair

- Height adjustable.
- Back/seat. adjustable.
- Stable, five-point base.
- Fully supports lower back (lumber support cushions are available).
- Optional arms.
- Optional back heights.

Desk

- Suitable size.
- Matt (non-reflective) surface.

Environment

- Comfortable.
- Sufficient working space.
- Not adversely affected by noise.
- Appropriate lighting levels for tasks.
- Equipment wires managed, eg in cable tidies.

Laptops

- Use on solid surface at correct keying height.
- Minimise prolonged use – take breaks.

Are the workers aware they:

- need to take regular breaks away from the DSE work;
- are entitled to free eye tests* and (if necessary) glasses?
* This applies to employees (operators) only but it is good practice to include volunteers as well.

Yes → Do workers take their breaks?

No

Yes → Keep under review.

Arrange awareness training for DSE workers to cover:

- workstation layout, including correct operating posture;
- DSE work breaks;
- procedure for organising eye tests and (if necessary) glasses.

Find out why not (eg pressure of work, poor management) and take appropriate action (eg software that monitors and enforces break compliance).

Table 14 Management checklist: Work equipment

Checkpoints	Yes, No or N/A	Action required	
		By whom?	By when?
Before purchasing work equipment (where applicable)			
Is it suitable for the intended use?			
Do the intended users have any special requirements, eg left-handed controls?			
Can it be located safely?			
Are there sufficient services, eg electricity, gas and/or water?			
Is there sufficient lighting and space to use it safely?			
Have you received safety information from the supplier or manufacturer?			
Are you aware of the hazards associated with the work equipment?			
Is there a maintenance and/or service agreement available to suit your needs, eg 24-hour call out?			
After purchasing work equipment			
Have your workers been trained to use the work equipment?			
Is there an easy-to-follow instruction manual?			
Is the work equipment for restricted, trained use only?			
Have you carried out an assessment of the risks associated with the work equipment?			
Are emergency and stop controls obvious and easy to use?			
Is the work equipment part of a planned preventative maintenance programme?			
Is the work equipment covered by a regular service agreement?			
Are the work equipment users aware of the associated hazards and how to avoid/reduce them?			
Is there a system for reporting and dealing with faulty equipment, such as removing it from use?			

Table 14 Management checklist: Work equipment (continued)

Checkpoints	Yes, No or N/A	Action required By whom?	By when?
Lifting equipment			
Have you identified all the lifting equipment and accessories in your workplace, eg passenger lifts, vehicle tail lifts, hoists, slings, pulleys, hooks and chains etc?			
Is the safe working load/limit clearly marked for each item?			
Is lifting equipment included in a detailed planned preventative maintenance programme?			
Is all your lifting equipment covered by scheduled thorough examinations and reports?			
Are workers trained to use the lifting equipment safely?			
Electrical equipment			
Is all portable electrical equipment PAT tested and clearly labelled as such?			
If permitted, do you include personal electrical items (eg radios) in your PAT system?			
Do workers carry out a visual check of cables and plugs before use?			
Are workers competent to carry out electrical maintenance work – this may mean access to fully qualified electricians?			
Are additional safety aids (such as RCDs) available – especially for off-site or external work?			
Can low-voltage electrical equipment be used, eg on construction sites?			
Is there a system for reporting and dealing with faulty equipment?			
Do any work activities involve the use of electrical equipment near water?			
Do any work activities involve the use of electrical equipment in high-risk areas (eg explosive atmospheres – special laws apply)? If yes, **get advice**.			
Are electrical items included in a planned preventative maintenance programme?			

Table 14 Management checklist: Work equipment (continued)

Checkpoints	Yes, No or N/A	Action required	
		By whom?	By when?
Noise			
Does the work equipment pose a risk from exposure to noise?			
Can the noise exposure be avoided?			
Have you assessed the noise risks?			
Can the noise be dampened, ie reduced?			
Can the noisy equipment be isolated?			
Can exposure times be reduced?			
Is there a health surveillance programme for monitoring worker hearing ability?			
Are work areas where daily personal noise exposures are 85 dB or above clearly marked as ear protection zones?			
Have suitable ear protection and storage facilities been provided?			
Vibration			
Does the work equipment pose a risk from exposure to vibration?			
Can the vibration exposure be avoided?			
If not, have you assessed the vibration type (eg hand-arm or whole-body vibration) and associated risks?			
Can the vibration be dampened, ie reduced?			
Can exposure times be reduced?			
Is there a health surveillance programme to monitor workers for the effects of vibration?			
Are workers aware of the ill-health effects of vibration and how to control them?			

Table 14 Management checklist: Work equipment (continued)

Checkpoints	Yes, No or N/A	Action required	
		By whom?	By when?
Display screen equipment			
Have you identified all of your workers who regularly use computers or other display screen equipment (DSE) at work?			
Have you identified workers who regularly use DSE for work purposes at home, ie homeworkers?			
Have workstation assessments been carried out for all workers, including homeworkers, who regularly use DSE for their work?			
Do the workstation assessments cover:			
■ computer screen; ■ keyboard/mouse; ■ accessories; ■ software; ■ chairs; ■ desks; ■ surrounding work environment; ■ laptop use.			
Have your workers been given training in understanding the risks associated with DSE use and how to prevent or control them?			
Do your workers know the need for them to take regular breaks away from DSE work?			
Do your workers actually take regular breaks away from DSE work?			
Are your DSE workers aware of their entitlement to free eye-sight tests and if necessary glasses?			

The workplace

214 Workplace health and safety covers a wide range of subjects that relate to the premises and actual location where the work activities are carried out. This is usually a building but may also be outside (as in farming, forestry etc) or work up a ladder (ie working at height). The associated health and safety issues are dependent on the type and location of the workplace.

215 The main law that covers workplaces is the Workplace (Health, Safety and Welfare) Regulations 1992 (the 'Workplace Regulations'). Asbestos, water, electricity and gas are covered by their own laws, and working at height is covered by the Work at Height Regulations 2005.

216 Workplaces can be split down into five main areas:

■ building structure;
■ fittings, eg doors and windows;
■ local working environment, eg seating, temperature, lighting, ventilation, space;
■ welfare, eg cleanliness, drinking water and rest and changing facilities;
■ building services, eg water, electricity and gas. You should also consider drainage systems.

217 The health and safety issues relevant to each of these and which should be covered by your risk assessment are listed in paragraphs 218-239.

Structure

218 Consider:

■ safety of the actual building structure;
■ the presence of asbestos;
■ integrity of firewalls, eg in roof/loft spaces;
■ entrances and exits, including changes in floor level such as steps, stairs or ramps.

219 The workplace buildings must be structurally sound, well maintained and safe, ie no broken or damaged walls etc. This means having a planned preventative maintenance programme in place to detect and put right any problems before they become a health and safety risk. This includes ensuring that any firewalls, especially in roof spaces, are not damaged during maintenance or wiring work. You need to have a procedure in place to check that these walls are not damaged after any work is carried out that may affect them.

Asbestos

220 It is also important to know what the building structure actually contains, eg asbestos or other hazardous substances, particularly if any refurbishment or alteration work is planned. The Control of Asbestos at Work Regulations 2005 (currently being reviewed) lay down strict controls on any work where there is a risk of exposure to asbestos. You have a duty to carry out an asbestos survey of your workplace to identify areas where asbestos is or could be present – at the simplest, this could be assuming that asbestos will be present if any building work is carried out, ie assume the worst-case scenario.

221 It is worth checking any building-related information and records to see if asbestos was actually used in the building and if so, where. You will need trained and competent people to do actual asbestos surveys – these will normally be specialised asbestos contractors. If asbestos is a possible issue in your workplace you need to read the asbestos-related guidance available from HSE.

Entrances and exits

222 The ways into and out of a workplace are as important as the actual place of work. You need to consider the safety of external roads and pathways, particularly in preventing slips on fallen leaves or ice, or trips or falls from uneven surfaces and potholes – this should be part of the premises maintenance programme. If vehicles and people use the same areas, how will you keep them separated?

223 Your entrances and exits should also allow for disabled use – this applies to the movement of disabled people around your building as well. Think about people with physical impairments, eg wheelchair users, as well as those with sensory impairments, eg blindness or deafness. Floor level changes need to be clearly marked in some way.

224 Stairways should be well lit, with at least one handrail and non-slip surfaces with a contrasting colour edge so visually impaired people are aware of the end of the step. Most stairways will be part of the building's fire escape routes and are what is called a 'protected zone'. This means they will have fire doors at the top and bottom and on any adjoining corridors and must be kept clear of any combustible materials and heat sources, ie the wells underneath stairs must not be used for storage.

Fittings

225 Consider:

- windows and areas of glazing, eg windows, skylights, patio doors;
- doors;
- floors and traffic routes.

Windows and glazing
226 Windows:

- should be able to be opened and closed safely, eg no stretching over wide window sills or having to reach up high. They should also open/close easily so no physical effort is needed;
- should prevent people from falling out while opening or closing the windows;
- once open, should not be a risk to anyone outside, eg they should not open out onto fire escapes or footpaths where people could walk into them;
- in some workplaces may need to be fitted with opening restrictors to windows above ground floor level, to prevent people falling or jumping out;
- should be able to be cleaned safely.

227 Glazing:

- should be impact-proof strengthened glass if it is in areas where people are likely to come into contact with it;
- should have some form of obvious marking on it to prevent people walking into it because it can't be seen.

Doors
228 The health and safety issues around doors will depend on the type and functions of the doors in your workplace. As a guide, you may need to consider:

- Can you see who is on the other side of the door, ie do the doors have vision panels? This is particularly important for doors that can be opened both ways (see Case study 51).
- Do electric doors have a fail-safe system so that in the event of a fault or power failure, they automatically unlock or open?
- Are there warning signs displayed on automatic doors saying which way they open? A mark on the ground to show where the doors open to should also be considered to prevent people walking into the opening doors.

- If self-closers are fitted, are the closing mechanisms adjusted so that the door does not shut too quickly and hit people?
- Are doors marked with 'push/pull' signs to show which way they open?

Floors and traffic routes
229 Again, there are a few simple points to think about:

- Do you have suitable, non-slip flooring in high slip risk areas, eg kitchens, laundries and workplaces where there is likely to be water or oil use and spillages?
- Floor surfaces should be well maintained, level and even – you need a system to report and repair areas of damage.
- Avoid the use of mats and rugs; they are trip hazards and tend to move as people walk over them.
- How are you controlling wet floor surfaces, eg from spillages or from people walking into the workplace if it is wet outside?
- Where possible, have separate and clearly marked routes for people and vehicles (see Driving and transport chapter).
- Plan how and when floor cleaning takes place. There are several 'dry' cleaning systems available that remove the need for a 'mop and bucket'. Avoid busy times and if possible, stop workers using the cleaned floors until they are dry, at the least, display clear warning signs (but make sure that the signs themselves do not become a trip risk).

Working environment

230 For indoor work environments, consider:

- available working space;
- temperature;
- ventilation;
- seating;
- noise;
- lighting;
- cleanliness and rubbish disposal.

231 Paragraph 230 lists the more common aspects of workplace health and safety, which are covered in other HSE guidance. In summary, the actual areas where workers carry out their work activities should be comfortable, safe and not pose a risk to their health.

232 There should be sufficient space for workers to do their job and for people to move around without knocking into other people or furniture etc. The work area should also be comfortable, ie not too hot or cold, not to noisy (remember, soft continuous noises may be as annoying and stressful as loud noises). Seating should be provided if it is possible to do work sitting down and must be suitable for the workers and for their tasks.

233 Lighting and ventilation should be suitable for the intended tasks and be by natural means where possible. High levels of lighting will be needed where precision tasks are carried out and for stairways. Good levels of ventilation will be needed in work environments such as kitchens, laundries, bathrooms, hydrotherapy or swimming pool areas.

234 Workplaces should be kept clean and tidy and have a good standard of decoration.

Welfare

235 The Workplace Regulations also cover the provision of welfare facilities for workers at work. Consider:

- toilets:
  - these may be unisex but must offer privacy to users;
  - they must be within reasonable distance to workplaces;
  - there must be sufficient numbers for the number of regular workers – recommendations are given in the Workplace Regulations ACOP;
- hand basins – with a means of cleaning and drying hands;
- rest rooms:
  - must be provided if a pregnant woman or a woman who has recently give birth requires them;
  - must also be protected from tobacco smoke – this may be achieved by providing separate rooms (smoking and non-smoking) or providing effective extraction of smoke fumes;
- changing rooms where workers have to change into/out of and keep their uniforms;
- provision of safe drinking water – this may be mains water outlets or cold water dispensers.

Services

236 You will also need to think about the services in your workplace. You should have procedures in place to ensure designated workers know where and how to turn off the service supply in emergencies (eg gas leaks) and how to contact the emergency services. Consider:

- safety of the building wiring systems – five-yearly checks are recommended;
- gas appliance safety – annual checks are required;
- water system safety, eg contamination by legionella bacteria, foreign bodies;
- effective drainage.

Outdoor workers

237 Your risk assessment must also cover any outdoor environments that your workers may have to work in. These may include fields, woods, parks, gardens, car parks, outside footpaths, patios, or roadways within the grounds etc. Essentially, all of the points identified in this chapter should be considered, eg providing toilets and hand-washing facilities, drinking water, the work environment.

Work at height

238 The nature of some work activities require them to be carried out at height. An example is window cleaning, although an elderly volunteer standing on a kick stool to reach items on a high shelf in a charity shop is also work at height.

239 You need to decide if the height at which the work is carried out is sufficient to cause injury if the worker fell. If it is, then you need to do a risk assessment and remove or reduce the risks. Where possible, work at height should be avoided. Ladders should not be considered the easy answer and again, should only be used if there is no other way of carrying out the work safely. Where ladders are used, there are strict safe practices to follow to ensure the ladder's stability.

Further information

Workplace health, safety and welfare. Workplace (Health, Safety and Welfare) Regulations 1992. Approved Code of Practice L24 HSE Books 1992 ISBN 0 7176 0413 6

Workplace health, safety and welfare: A short guide for managers Leaflet INDG244 HSE Books 1997 (single copy free or priced packs of 10 ISBN 0 7176 1328 3)

Officewise Leaflet INDG173 HSE Books 1994 (single copy free or priced packs of 10 ISBN 0 7176 1518 9)

Preventing slips and trips at work Leaflet INDG225(rev1) HSE Books 2003 (single copy free or priced packs of 15 ISBN 0 7176 2760 8)

Slip assessment tool: available online at www.hse.gov.uk/slips. (You will need access to a surface roughness measuring device to use this assessment tool – many HSE enforcing offices will these devices and be able to assist.)

Homeworking: Guidance for employers and employees on health and safety Leaflet INDG226 HSE Books 1996 (single copy free or priced packs of 15 ISBN 0 7176 1204 X)

Welfare at work: Guidance for employers on welfare provisions Leaflet INDG293 HSE Books 1999 (single copy free)

HSE's temperature and thermal comfort website www.hse.gov.uk/temperature

Lighting at work HSG38 (Second edition) HSE Books 1997 ISBN 0 7176 1232 5

Seating at work HSG57 (Second edition) HSE Books 1997 ISBN 0 7176 1231 7

Slips and trips: Guidance for employers on identifying hazards and controlling risks HSG155 HSE Books 1996 ISBN 0 7176 1145 0

Health and safety in care homes HSG220 HSE Books 2001 ISBN 0 7176 2082 4

Legionnaires' disease. The control of legionella bacteria in water systems. Approved Code of Practice and guidance L8 (Third edition) HSE Books 2000 ISBN 0 7176 1772 6

Legionnaires' disease: A guide for employers IAC27REV2 HSE Books 2001 ISBN 0 7176 1773 4

Controlling legionella in nursing and residential care homes Leaflet INDG253 HSE Books 1997 (single copy free)

A comprehensive guide to managing asbestos in premises HSG227 HSE Books 2002 ISBN 0 7176 2381 5

Case study 50: Lighting

Volunteers working in a busy office noticed an increase in headaches and ill health following relocation to a new site. There was a reduction in the natural light available and the strip lights appeared rather dim.

Hazards
- Poor lighting.
- Workload.

Harm
- Increased sickness:
  - eyestrain;
  - headaches;
  - general ill heath.
- Increased sickness absence.
- Poor morale.

Solutions
- Ensure the layout of the office maximises the use of natural light.
- Check the type and capacity of the current lighting.
- Seek advice for suppliers on the recommended types and their location to ensure effective spread.
- Ensure lights are cleaned periodically to maintain the lighting level.
- Seek further qualified support if the problem persists.

Case study 51: Vision panels in fire doors

A charity had a strong 'poster culture', ie advertising the latest campaign or emergency by sticking posters up throughout the offices, especially on the vision panels in fire doors and other internal doors. This resulted in a number of collisions and minor injuries (although the potential was there for a more serious injury, especially at the top of stairwells).

Hazards
- Obstructed vision panels.

Harm
- Collision accidents.
- Breach of fire regulations.
- Putting staff at risk in the event of a fire – delayed evacuation.

Solutions
- Discussion with the main departments responsible for promoting their activities via this means.
- Agreement on where posters could not be displayed for safety reasons.
- Identify areas where posters could safely be displayed (eg staff notice boards, kitchen areas) and provide extra notice boards to encourage this.
- Agreement that all notices on vision panels would be removed by the facilities department and disposed of, so reducing the impact of the communication strategy (ie less posters).
- Encourage use of staff newsletters, team meetings etc to pass on information.

Case study 52: Storage

The publicity department on the first floor would regularly order very large quantities of publicity/campaigning materials but did not have sufficient storage space. Deliveries were left on any available floor space near the ground floor reception, often in corridors and in front of fire exits. Later, when room was found, the boxes were moved to the first floor office.

Hazards
- Moving and handling loads.
- Obstructed corridors and fire doors.
- Fire.
- Bad image and first impressions for visitors entering the building.

Harm
- Trips and falls to workers and visitors.
- Back and other injuries caused by moving the materials.

Solutions
- Review storage space.
- Order only what is needed at any one time.
- Arrange for materials to be delivered to the first floor direct.
- Receptionists instructed not to accept deliveries left on the ground floor.

Notes
1   Storage is an issue in every workplace – there is never enough. Effective management of stock and regular review and disposal of stored items and records is therefore important.

Case study 53: Temperature

During winter months workers complained that the office was cold and draughty. They brought in portable heaters from home, some of them very old. This led to a shortage of electrical sockets, so they started to use extension leads. One of the heaters was left on at the end of the working day, and it was only by chance that this was discovered by a cleaner early the next morning. The cleaner reported that the fire had got very hot, and that files close by were also very warm to the touch.

Hazards
- Faulty equipment.
- Fire.
- Trip hazards from trailing leads.

Harm
- Electric shock or electrocution.
- Injuries and premises damage due to fire.
- Low staff morale if minimum work environment standards not met.
- Staff absences.
- Civil and criminal charges.
- Damaged reputation and loss of business.

Solutions
- Prohibit the use of personal electrical equipment in the workplace, but ensure that equipment supplied by the employer is fit for use (see *Work equipment* chapter).
- Regular servicing of heating equipment, including annual PAT testing on electrical appliances.
- Monitoring temperatures to ensure minimum standard for temperature (16 °C for seated or stationery workers and 13 °C for workers carrying out physical activities).
- Providing safe supplementary heaters where appropriate, with instructions for safe use and siting.
- Strictly enforced shutdown routine at the end of each working day to turn off and unplug all electrical equipment.

Notes
1   While there are recommended minimum temperatures for workplaces, there are no recommended maximum temperatures. Hot temperatures can cause a range of adverse health effects, which need different control measures, and which may be influenced by nearby heat sources, air flow, physical activity, clothing and individual tolerances/comfort levels. If workers start to experience adverse health effects due to feeling too hot (eg significant sweating, dehydration, heat fatigue or heat stroke) then action is needed to control and reduce temperatures. Examples where hot temperatures could be a problem are kitchens, laundries and boiler houses. Care homes and hospitals may also have higher than normal working temperatures for the comfort of residents or patients.
2   Temperatures are also important for workers who work outside. You will need to provide proper personal protective clothing for cold or wet weather and have procedures to protect workers from sun exposure in the summer.
3   HSE has a 'temperature' section on its website, with information on thermal risk assessments and further guidance on the subject: www.hse.gov.uk/temperature/thermal.

Case study 54: Work at height

A window cleaner is contracted to clean the windows of a charity's office on the first floor of an old Victorian house.

Hazards
- Falls from height.

Harm
- Injuries associated with falling from height, eg serious fractures, unconsciousness.

Solutions
- Ensure the window cleaning company is reputable and competent for the intended work, especially if specialised equipment is needed – ask for and follow up references.
- Ask for a copy of their risk assessment and method statement (this explains how they intend to carry out their work on your premises).
- Avoid use of ladders whenever possible, eg use a mechanical arm (cherry picker), water-fed poles or telescopic handles or have reversible windows that can be cleaned from the inside.
- Agree first-aid arrangements, ie will the window cleaners use the charity's first aiders.
- If ladders have to be used, agree who will provide them and ensure the procedures for safe ladder use are followed.
- Ensure the premises are as safe as possible and that the contractor is aware of any hazards associated with the areas they will be working in.

Notes
1   You can include/impose conditions of work in your contract with the window cleaners, eg that the use of ladders should be avoided and that risk assessments must be provided.
2   The contract should also detail who will provide the equipment needed to carry out the work. If the charity provides any equipment, they will be responsible and liable for the safety and maintenance of that equipment (eg ladders) and that they are used safely.

Case study 55: Asbestos

A charity maintenance worker is sent into one of the charity's shops, built during the 1950s, to fix a leaking hot water pipe. To get to the actual leak, the maintenance worker has to cut through some of the ceiling tiles and remove the pipe lagging.

Hazards
- Exposure to asbestos fibres.
- Work at height.
- Dangers associated with work equipment.
- Exposure to legionella bacteria.

Harm
- Asbestos-related illnesses (maintenance worker, shop workers and customers).
- Injuries from falling.
- Injuries/ill health associated with type and use of work equipment.
- Infections, eg legionellosis, including legionnaires' disease.
- Loss of business due to closure for asbestos removal.

Solutions
- Confirm with property landlord whether an asbestos survey has been carried out and what type; if not you will need to know where asbestos is (or is likely to be) and whether your workers and customers are at risk from asbestos exposure, both from the area you have control over and from the rest of the premises.
- Identify and mark on a plan possible high-risk asbestos sites within the shop. HSE guidance provides easy-to-follow information on common high-risk asbestos locations within buildings.
- Train your maintenance workers to identify possible asbestos sites so they are aware of associated dangerous locations and can avoid asbestos exposure; this will not make them competent or qualified to remove asbestos. Removal must only be carried out by a recognised and registered asbestos removal company.

Notes
1   Asbestos is not dangerous until it becomes damaged and fibres are released into the air. If asbestos is present and is (and remains) in a good and undamaged state, it does not need to be removed.

2   If the premises have not had an asbestos survey, you will need to liaise and agree for one to be undertaken with the shop landlord; you may be liable if your workers are exposed to asbestos and you have not taken any steps to ensure their health and safety, even if the premises are not under your direct control. Check with other local charity shops to see if there is a 'friendly' asbestos company that can offer good rates for the asbestos work.

Case study 56: Slips, trips and falls

A visitor to the main reception of a charity slipped on the floor in the reception area, after coming in from the rain. The visitor broke his arm in the fall and was taken to hospital by ambulance.

Hazards
- Floor surface.
- Outside conditions (rain).

Harm
- Broken arm.
- Bad publicity.

Solutions
- Protect the area immediately outside the doors from rain, eg protruding door canopies.
- Ensure effective premises maintenance programmes are in place so drains do not become blocked and/or gutters damaged etc (this may increase the amount of water outside the building that people have to work through).
- Identify high-risk slip areas and provide suitable flooring or other means of removing water from footwear, eg door mats. Make sure items such as doormats do not increase the risks, ie by becoming a trip hazard.
- Have systems in place to clean up excess surface water.
- Review the accident reports to see if there are any common trends or conditions that may suggest a cause or show if the problem is becoming worse.
- Report the accident under RIDDOR (see the *Accidents* chapter). RIDDOR applies because a member of the public was injured and taken directly to hospital for treatment.

Notes
1   Advice on the level of slip risks and possible control measures is available from HSE's *Slips Assessment Tool* on the HSE website (www.hse.gov.uk/slips).

2   If doormats are provided, they should be secured into position and should be large enough to remove most of the water from footwear.

3   Flooring manufacturers are able to give advice on suitable flooring types and ways of treating existing floor surfaces to increase the slip resistance.

Figure 14 Workplace flow chart

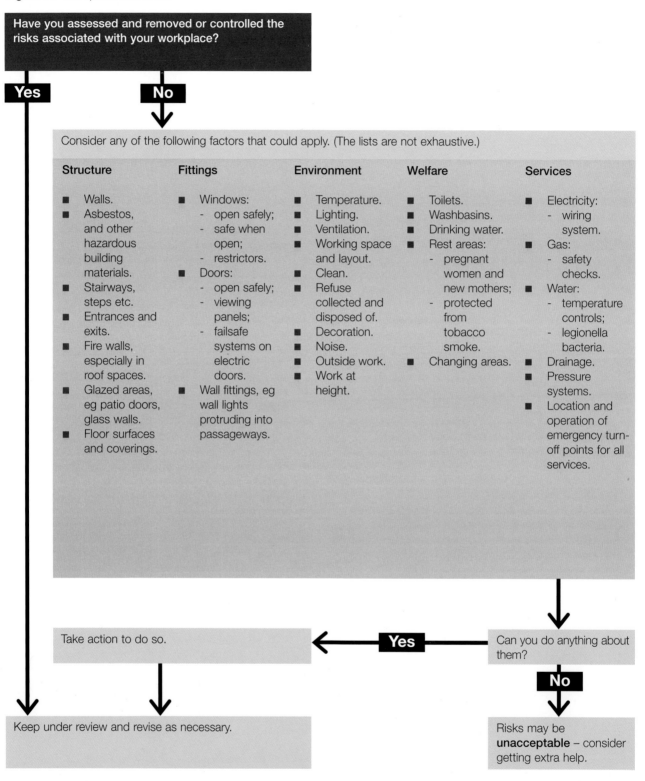

Have you assessed and removed or controlled the risks associated with your workplace?

Yes

No

Consider any of the following factors that could apply. (The lists are not exhaustive.)

Structure	Fittings	Environment	Welfare	Services

■ Walls.
■ Asbestos, and other hazardous building materials.
■ Stairways, steps etc.
■ Entrances and exits.
■ Fire walls, especially in roof spaces.
■ Glazed areas, eg patio doors, glass walls.
■ Floor surfaces and coverings.
	■ Windows:
	  - open safely;
	  - safe when open;
	  - restrictors.
	■ Doors:
	  - open safely;
	  - viewing panels;
	  - failsafe systems on electric doors.
	■ Wall fittings, eg wall lights protruding into passageways.
		■ Temperature.
		■ Lighting.
		■ Ventilation.
		■ Working space and layout.
		■ Clean.
		■ Refuse collected and disposed of.
		■ Decoration.
		■ Noise.
		■ Outside work.
		■ Work at height.
			■ Toilets.
			■ Washbasins.
			■ Drinking water.
			■ Rest areas:
			  - pregnant women and new mothers;
			  - protected from tobacco smoke.
			■ Changing areas.
				■ Electricity:
				  - wiring system.
				■ Gas:
				  - safety checks.
				■ Water:
				  - temperature controls;
				  - legionella bacteria.
				■ Drainage.
				■ Pressure systems.
				■ Location and operation of emergency turn-off points for all services.

Take action to do so.

Yes

Can you do anything about them?

No

Keep under review and revise as necessary.

Risks may be **unacceptable** – consider getting extra help.

Table 14 Management checklist: Workplace

Checkpoints	Yes, No or N/A	Action required	
		By whom?	By when?
The premises			
Is there a named person responsible for managing the premises?			
Is there an inspection and maintenance programme to cover gas, electrics, water supplies and drainage?			
Is there a system for managing asbestos?			
Is all low-level glass in windows/doors made of safety material or protected by a barrier?			
Are there secure handrails on staircases/steps?			
Are corridors and exit doors kept clear?			
Is the building accessible to disabled people?			
Are there arrangements for managing contractors working on site?			
Is security adequate – with a signing in and out system for visitors?			
Fire safety			
Is there a current fire risk assessment for the building? (See chapter *Fire safety*.)			
Does the emergency plan identify the location of emergency cut off points?			
The working environment			
Have risk assessments been carried out at individual workstations. (See chapter *Work equipment*.)			
Is there enough space for people to work in comfort and to move around safely?			
Is the lighting, heating and ventilation adequate?			
Is the workplace uncomfortably noisy?			
Are there arrangements for cleaning and disposing of waste?			
Are there any special activities that need to be assessed separately (eg working at height, lone working, outside work)?			

Table 14 Management checklist: Workplace (continued)

Checkpoints	Yes, No or N/A	Action required	
		By whom?	By when?
Welfare facilities			
Are there enough toilet and hand-washing facilities?			
Are there facilities for making hot drinks?			
Is drinking water available?			
Is there a rest area, especially for pregnant and nursing mothers? Is there protection from tobacco smoke?			
Is there storage for outdoor clothing and other personal belongings?			
Is there a first-aid box and qualified first aider?			

Appendix 1: Useful contacts

1   This section includes details of organisations that have agreed to provide advice or other help to charities in the management of their health, safety and welfare arrangements. In many cases the websites of these organisations, such as HSE, IOSH, RoSPA and CSG, will have examples of good practice and sources of practical help. Your local library may have access to the Internet.

Health and Safety Executive (HSE)

RIDDOR
Incident Contact Centre (ICC)
Caerphilly Business Park
Caerphilly
CF83 3GG
Tel: 0845 300 9923
Fax: 0845 300 9924
Website: www.riddor.gov.uk

General (for information about health and safety)
Infoline
HSE Information Services
Caerphilly Business Park
Caerphilly
CF83 3GG
Tel: 0845 345 0055
Fax: 0845 408 9566
Textphone: 0845 408 9577
E-mail: hse.infoline@natbrit.com
Website: www.hse.gov.uk

Publications
HSE priced and free publications are available by mail order from HSE Books. HSE priced publications are also available from bookshops and free leaflets can be downloaded from HSE's website: www.hse.gov.uk.

HSE Books
PO Box 1999
Sudbury
Suffolk CO10 2WA
Tel: 01787 881165
Fax: 01787 313995
Website: www.hsebooks.co.uk

Charities Safety Group (CSG)
Old Brompton Road
Box 541
London SW7 3SS
Tel: 07745 937567
E-mail: csginfo@ncvo-vol.org.uk
Website: www.csg.org.uk

Institute of Occupational Safety and Health (IOSH)
The Grange
Highfield Drive
Wigston
Leicestershire LE18 1NN
Tel: 0116 257 3100
Fax: 0116 257 3101
Website: www.iosh.co.uk

Royal Society for the Prevention of Accidents (RoSPA)
RoSPA House
Edgbaston House
353 Bristol Road
Edgbaston
Birmingham B5 7ST
Tel: 0121 248 2000
Fax: 0121 248 2001
E-mail: help@rospa.com
Website: www.rospa.co.uk

National Health and Safety Groups Council – details and contact through the RoSPA website 'search' link

Chartered Institute of Environmental Health (CIEH)
Chadwick Court
15 Hatfields
London SE1 8DJ
Tel: 020 7928 6006
Fax: 020 7827 5862
E-mail: info@cieh.org
Website: www.cieh.org.uk

Other useful contacts

National Council for Voluntary Organisations (NCVO)
Regent's Wharf
8 All Saints Street
London N1 9RL
Tel: 020 7713 6161
Fax: 020 7713 6300
E-mail: ncvo@ncvo-vol.org.uk
Website: www.ncvo-vol.org.uk

Upkeep – including Charities Facilities Management Group (CFMG)
The Building Centre
26 Store Street
London WC1E 7BT
Tel: 020 7631 1677
Fax: 020 7631 1699
E-mail: info@upkeep.org.uk
Website: www.upkeep.org.uk

Contact CFMG via e-mail to Annette McGill:
info@upkeep.org.uk

Westminster City Council – Environmental Health Department
(CSG LAPS partner)
PO Box 240
Westminster City Hall
64 Victoria Street
London SW1E 6QP
Tel: 020 7641 6000
Fax: 020 7245 5510
Website: www.westminster.gov.uk

(Please note that all LAPS enquires must be made through CSG in the first instance.)

Association of Charity Shops
Central House
14 Upper Woban Place
London WC1H 0AE
Tel: 020 7255 4470
E-mail: mail@charityshops.org.uk
Website: www.charityshops.org.uk

The Suzy Lamplugh Trust
National Centre for Personal Safety
Hampton House
20 Albert Embankment
London SE1 7TJ
Tel: 020 8876 0305
Fax: 020 8876 0891
E-mail: info@suzylamplugh.org.uk
Website: www.suzylamplugh.org.uk

BACKCARE
16 Elmtree Road
Teddington
Middlesex TW11 8ST
Tel: 020 8977 5474
Fax: 020 8943 5318
E-mail: info@backcare.org.uk
Website: www.backcare.org.uk

International Aid Trust
Longton Business Park
Station Road
Much Hoole
Preston
Lancashire PR4 5LE
Tel: 01772 611000
Fax: 01772 619933
E-mail: office@internationalaidtrust.org.uk
Website: www.internationalaidtrust.org.uk

Office of the Deputy Prime Minister (ODPM) – UK Fire Policy
Eland House
Bressenden Place
London SW1E 5DU
Tel: 020 7944 4400
Fax: 020 7944 9645
E-mail: enquiryodpm@odpm.gsi.gov.uk
Website: odpm.gov.uk

Trades Union Congress (TUC)
Congress House
Great Russell Street
London WC1B 3LS
Tel: 020 7636 4030
Fax: 020 7636 0632
Website: www.tuc.org.uk

Unison
1 Mabledon Place
London WC1H 9AJ
Tel: 0845 355 0845
Website: www.unison.org.uk

Regional offices can be contacted via links from website
home page.

Amicus
Head Office
35 King Street
Covent Garden
London WC2E 8JG
Tel (membership and administration): 0800 587 1222
Website: www.amicustheunion.org.uk

British Retail Consortium
2nd Floor
21 Dartmouth Street
London SW1H 9BP
Tel: 020 7854 8900
Fax: 020 7854 8901
Website: www.brc.org.uk

*National Inspection Council for Electrical Installation
Contracting (NICEIC)*
Warwick House
Houghton Hall Park
Houghton Regis
Dunstable
Bedfordshire LU5 5ZX
Tel: 01582 531000
Fax: 01582 531010
Website: www.niceic.org.uk

British Association of Removers
Tangent House
62 Exchange Road
Watford
Hertfordshire WD18 0TG
Tel: 01923 699480
Fax: 01923 699481
E-mail: info@bar.co.uk
Website: www.removers.org.uk

British Association for Counselling and Psychotherapy
BACP House
35-37 Albert Street
Rugby
Warwickshire CV21 2SG
Tel: 0870 443 5252
Fax: 0870 443 5161
E-mail: bacp.co.uk
Website: www.bacp.co.uk

Victim Support
National Office (England)
Cranmer House
39 Brixton road
London SW9 6DZ
Tel: 020 7735 9166
Fax: 020 7582 5712
Victim Supportline: 0845 3030900
E-mail: contact@victimsupport.org.uk
Website: www.victimsupport.org.uk

Food Standards Agency
UK Headquarters
Aviation House
125 Kingsway
London WC2B 6NH
Tel: 020 7276 8000
Website: www.food.gov.uk

Contact details for the following organisations can be found
in the local phone books:

The Samaritans
Crime Prevention Officers
Fire Brigades

Appendix 2: Relevant legislation

1   Legislation mentioned in this publication is listed below. Other health and safety legislation may apply to your organisation.

2   The Stationery Office publications are available from The Stationery Office, PO Box 29, Norwich NR3 1GN Tel: 0870 600 5522 Fax: 0870 600 5533 e-mail: customer.services@tso.co.uk Website: www.tso.co.uk (They are also available from bookshops.)

Control of Asbestos at Work Regulations 2002 SI 2002/2675 The Stationery Office 2002 ISBN 0 11 042918 4

Control of Noise at Work Regulations 2005 SI 2005/1643 The Stationery Office 2005 ISBN 0 11 072984 6

Control of Substances Hazardous to Health Regulations 2002 SI 2002/2677 The Stationery Office 2002 ISBN 0 11 042919 2 (as amended)

Control of Vibration at Work Regulations 2005 SI 2005/1093 The Stationery Office 2005 ISBN 0 11 072767 3

Data Protection Act 1998 Ch29 The Stationery Office 1998 ISBN 0 10 542998 8

Electricity at Work Regulations 1989 SI 1989/635 The Stationery Office 1989 ISBN 0 11 096635 X

Employers' Liability (Compulsory Insurance) Act 1969 Ch57 The Stationery Office 1969 ISBN 0 10 545769 8

Health and Safety at Work etc Act 1974 Ch37 The Stationery Office 1974 ISBN 0 10 543774 3

Health and Safety (Consultation with Employees) Regulations 1996 SI 1996/1513 The Stationery Office 1996 ISBN 0 11 054839 6

Health and Safety (Display Screen Equipment) Regulations 1992 SI 1992/2792 The Stationery Office 1992 ISBN 0 11 025919 X

Health and Safety (First Aid) Regulations 1981 SI 1981/917 The Stationery Office 1981 ISBN 0 11 016917 4

Health and Safety (Safety Signs and Signals) Regulations 1996 SI 1996/341 The Stationery Office 1996 ISBN 0 11 054093 X

Lifting Operations and Lifting Equipment Regulations 1998 SI 1998/2307 The Stationery Office 1998 ISBN 0 11 079598 9

Management of Health and Safety at Work Regulations 1999 SI 1999/3242 The Stationery Office 1999 ISBN 0 11 085625 2

Manual Handling Operations Regulations 1992 SI 1992/2793 The Stationery Office 1992 ISBN 0 11 025920 3 (as amended)

Provision and Use of Work Equipment Regulations 1998 SI 1998/2306 The Stationery Office 1998 ISBN 0 11 079599 7

Safety Representatives and Safety Committees Regulations 1977 SI 1977/500 The Stationery Office 1977 ISBN 0 11 070500 9

Workplace (Health, Safety and Welfare Regulations 1992 SI 1992/3004 The Stationery Office 1992 ISBN 0 11 025804 5

Appendix 3: Forms

Sample accident/incident reporting form

HSE form F2508: Report of an injury or dangerous occurence

Health and Safety at Work etc Act 1974
The Reporting of Injuries, Diseases and Dangerous Occurrences Regulations 1995

Report of an injury or dangerous occurrence

Filling in this form
This form must be filled in by an employer or other responsible person.

Part A

About you

1 What is your full name?

2 What is your job title?

3 What is your telephone number?

About your organisation

4 What is the name of your organisation?

5 What is its address and postcode?

6 What type of work does the organisation do?

Part B

About the incident

1 On what date did the incident happen?

2 At what time did the incident happen?
(Please use the 24-hour clock eg 0600)

3 Did the incident happen at the above address?

Yes ☐ Go to question 4

No ☐ Where did the incident happen?

☐ elsewhere in your organisation – give the name, address and postcode

☐ at someone else's premises – give the name, address and postcode

☐ in a public place – give details of where it happened

If you do not know the postcode, what is the name of the local authority?

4 In which department, or where on the premises, did the incident happen?

F2508 (05.00)

Part C

About the injured person

If you are reporting a dangerous occurrence, go to Part F. If more than one person was injured in the same incident, please attach the details asked for in Part C and Part D for each injured person.

1 What is their full name?

2 What is their home address and postcode?

3 What is their home phone number?

4 How old are they?

5 Are they
☐ male?
☐ female?

6 What is their job title?

7 Was the injured person (tick only one box)
☐ one of your employees?
☐ on a training scheme? Give details:

☐ on work experience?
☐ employed by someone else? Give details of the employer:

☐ self-employed and at work?
☐ a member of the public?

Part D

About the injury

1 What was the injury? (eg fracture, laceration)

2 What part of the body was injured?

ACCIDENT/INCIDENT REPORT FORM
To be completed and returned to the Health and Safety Department

Reporting Dept: .... Ref No (to be completed by Health and Safety Dept): ....

This form is to be used for reporting all injury accidents and non-injury incidents involving any person and that is associated with any of the organisation's activities and/or premises. This form must be completed and signed by the affected person (except where the affected person cannot do so themselves, when the reporting members of staff must complete the form) and the reporting department manager. The information must be legible (print), accurate, as detailed as possible and factual. Please use **black** ink. Boxes 1, 2, 3, 7 and 8 must be completed in all cases.

* Delete as appropriate

Accident/incident details | 1

Date: ....…   Time (24-hour clock): ....…Work related: Y/N*

Location details
Place and address of incident:
(please tick and provide address)

Main premises	☐
Off-site premises	☐
Shops	☐
Private home	☐
Off-site event	☐

Exact location of incident:

Description of incident

Please continue on and attach separate sheet if necessary.

Apparent cause (please tick) | 2

Abscondence (missing person)	☐	Moving and handling (not a person)	☐
Assault	☐	Moving object, struck by	☐
Animals	☐	Moving vehicle, struck by	☐
Biological agent, contact with	☐	Needlesticks	☐
Chemicals, contact with	☐	Sharps (other than needlesticks)	☐
Drug incidents	☐	Slip/trip	☐
Electricity, contact with	☐	Stationary object, struck against	☐
Equipment/machinery failure or misuse	☐	Structure/building/premises	☐
Fall from height	☐	Theft	☐
Fall on level	☐	Trip	☐
Fire/explosion	☐	Vehicle, driving	☐
Gas incident	☐	Vehicle, other	☐
Hot surfaces/water, contact with	☐	Miscellaneous/unknown	☐
Moving and handling a person	☐	Other (please specify):	☐

Affected person details   **3**

Did the incident involve a person: Y/N (if YES continue below: if NO then continue to Boxes 4 and 7)

Surname: First name(s):   Title:

Status: Agency / Contractor / Employee / Patient / Public / Unclassified / Visitor / Volunteer

Contact address:

Post code: Tel:

Date of birth: Age (if under 16 years):   Female/Male

a) Job title: b) ON/OFF duty at time

Witnesses   **4**

Name: Name:

Address/Phone no: Address/Phone no:

Status: Status:

Written statement: Y/N   Written statement: Y/N

Injury/treatment detail   **5**

Injury details   **Treatment details**
        (to be completed by doctor or first aider)

Description of injury: Treatment given:

Immediate treatment given:

Name (print):   Status:
        Name (print):

Signature:

Referred to:* [N/A] / Hospice doctor / GP / Hospital / Occupational health / Other (give details)

Notification details   **6**

Contact *(tick as appropriate)*
Name: **Date:**   **Time:**

Next of kin   ☐
Department manager   ☐
GP/hospital   ☐
Other *(please specify)*   ☐

Form completed by   **7**
(if not affected person)

Name:

Occupation:

Address:

Manager's report   **8**

Severity:* Near-miss / Minor / Significant / Serious
Action taken to prevent recurrence:

Name: **Signature:**   **Date:**

Health and safety report   **9**

Action: **Date:**
Accident report received...
Recorded (on computer)...
Investigated (date/by)...
RIDDOR reported (date)..
RIDDOR reported (method)......................................

Signature: **Date:**

R59066

Printed on recycled paper

Printed and published by the Health and Safety Executive   C60   07/06